Lawmen Unmasked

Heroes, Scoundrels, & The Famous Fighting Pimp

by **Jesse Wolf Hardin**

Foreword by **Boge Quinn** • Introduction by **John Taffin**

Author Hardin gives us a detailed look at the complex lives of 11 of the most fascinating Sheriffs and Marshals of the historic American West – from the con-artist and pimp Wyatt Earp to the true and often unsung heroes who so bravely wore the star.

**Burton Mossman • Wyatt Earp • Harry Morse • Bucky O'Neill
John Joshua Webb • Wild Bill Hickok • Pat Garrett • Bat Masterson
George Scarborough • Bear River Tom Smith • Elfego Baca**

"The passion and fun of living the Wild West lifestyle oozes off of every page. Here's to a pard who describes his passion as 'a glad ache for the frontier past'… Amen, etc."
-Bob Boze Bell
Editor, *True West Magazine*

Contents

Since we were kids, we've thrilled to the feats of Hollywood's heart-throbs,
and recoiled from the dastardly misdeeds of the outlaws in Western novels.
Only one problem... it seldom went down thataway!
Things were a lot more complex – and compared to these 1959 Warner actors,
a lot less black & white. Real, unslanted history, is even more compelling
than anything novelists and screenwriters could ever make up.
And more admirable than the white-hatted characters we see on the screen,
are those genuine heroes with or without a badge who prove willing
to stand up and pay the price to do what's right.

–Jesse Wolf Hardin

Boge Quinn and his brother Deacon Jeff produce one of the very most informative firearms sites on the web, GunBlast.com. *Boge is one of my favorite outdoor writers, an artist, bluegrass and gospel picker who tells it like it is. His warm manner, honest appraisals, sense of history, aesthetics and justice make him an ideal person to write a Foreword for this book.*

Foreword

by **Boge Quinn**

Jess Hardin is my kind of fellow. He is a knowledgeable historian, an accomplished poet, a skilled writer, an expert marksman, an able outdoorsman, a talented musician, and a gifted artist (the final two distinctions being particularly close to my heart. Jess possesses the rare ability to teach us how to hunt; why we hunt; how to use the weapons of the hunt; how to appreciate the techniques of hunting; how to cook what is hunted; and entertain us greatly while we learn from his experiences.

Some might consider *Lawmen of The Old West Unmasked* to be revisionist history, or that it indicates a lack of proper respect for those who made their living enforcing (or, in some cases, not enforcing or selectively enforcing) the law, but this would be a mistake on the reader's part. Jess Hardin only seeks to tell the truth within these pages. Truth is all too often not precisely recorded in history books, and certainly not fully and accurately portrayed by Hollywood. I see Jess' work more as an honest and refreshing portrayal of Lawmen as just that: as *men*, complete with the foibles and imperfections that plague us all. Among any given group of people, one will find the virtuous and the vile; the courageous and the cowardly; the pure and the polluted; the saint and the sinner. Jess Hardin does not seek to destroy the reputations of historical figures whom we have held dear for so long, but he explores the human side of the legendary, and the lesser-known, Lawmen who helped forge the past into the present.

Jess touches on not just the actions of these great men of history, but also upon their motivations, leaving the reader with much to contemplate: do the actions of a man make him great, or his motivations? A man's actions are what propel history, but his often-private motivations are what propel those actions.

This ability to draw the reader's mind into deeper contemplation is one of the hallmarks of a great historical work, and when coupled with Jess' accessible and appealing writing style, creates a work of historical importance.

Here at Gunblast.com, we have been pleased to publish a few articles from Jess, as well as some excerpts from his excellent book, *Old Guns and Whispering Ghosts*. Over the past few years, I have developed a nice friendship of correspondence with Jess Hardin. Although I have yet to meet him face-to-face, this is a situation which I hope to correct in the not-too-distant future. I would very much like to share a campfire, a beverage, and a fine cigar with him while we exchange tales of bygone days.

Unlike the actors in the previous poster, these fellows
are all the read deal – some genuine lawmen,
truly adept pistoleros, and straight talking scribes:

Bob Baer • John Taffin • John Wooters • Bart Skelton • Sheriff Jim Wilson

John Taffin is for the 21st Century what Elmer Keith was for an earlier generation, the #1 champion of the storied sixgun, and a wordsmith whose Western flavored "Campfire Tales" could inspire just about anyone. John is the author of untold columns in Guns Magazine, American Handgunner, Gun Digest *and more, as well as the author of a number of dandy books including* Big Bore Sixguns, Gun Digest Book of The .44, Book of the .45, *and* Action Shooting Cowboy Style:*www.sixguns.com*

John Taffin

Introduction

by **John Taffin**

My whole generation grew up being deceived. First there were the old West "B" movies which portrayed unreality to the limit. Everyone did not carry a sixgun in every town in the old West and certainly so-called heroes could not shoot a gun out of someone's hand and especially not do it without any harm coming to the recipient of a bullet. Hats could not be shot off heads and the number of actual gunfights with two men standing and facing each other on Main Street can be counted on the thumb of one hand. Fast draw and waiting for the other fellow to go for his sixgun first is purely imaginative Hollywood hokum. Hollywood also invented the so-called fast draw holster, in fact Arvo Ojala called his creation the Hollywood Fast Draw Holster. Of course Hollywood didn't stop with all of this but went on to singing cowboys, heroes dressed to the hilt carrying two ivory-gripped sixguns in fancy carved leather and riding beautiful horses almost as smart as they were.

We could easily forgive Hollywood for all of this simply in the name of entertainment for easily impressed youngsters. However, they didn't stop there. They often, more often than not, made heroes out of those who didn't even come close to being as portrayed on the screen. Truth is not only stranger than fiction, it is a whole lot more interesting. But Hollywood pretty much stayed with fiction. In the movie "Sunset" with James Garner playing an aging Wyatt Earp and consultant to a movie being made with Bruce Willis as Tom Mix who is portraying Wyatt Earp for the film. When Willis/Mix/Earp asks Garner/Earp whether that's the way it really happened the reply is "Give or take a lie or two." Well there were a whole lot more lies in Hollywood movies than one or two. Movies about Wyatt Earp are classic examples and then when the TV series "The Life and Legend of Wyatt Earp" appeared on TV it definitely should have had a disclaimer saying "any resemblance to persons living or dead is purely coincidental."

Wyatt Earp was portrayed as the epitome of virtue and honesty something he never ever came close to as we see in Jesse Hardin's book. Jesse strips away the lies and gives us a true picture of eleven "Lawmen of The Old West" and as he adds to the title, "Unmasked". Most of them do not come out looking anything like they have been portrayed. All of them were human beings with failings, none were perfect, except some were perfectly bad. Here we see the real Wyatt Earp, along with others who were portrayed on TV as I was growing up such as Elfego Baca, Bat Masterson, and Wild Bill Hickok. None of which in real life were as portrayed on TV. Entertaining? Yes. Factual? Not even close. Add in such other interesting characters as Bucky O'Neill, who served as a Rough Rider, Pat Garrett who betrayed a friend, and other tough lawmen such as Harry Morse, John Joshua Webb, Burt Mossman, Tom Smith, and also George Scarborough who is known as the last of the old-time gunmen, and it makes for a most interesting read.

I quote from chapter 10: "There are many who feel the need to tell only a partial story, to whitewash facts or sanitize the image of historical characters in order to be able to celebrate their lives... It bears repeating, that the Old West – and life itself – was never so clear-cut as some would have it. It was often only a disproportionately heavy application of power and the threat or actuality of violence that pulled in the reins on rampant criminal depredations, and the men who wielded that power were almost without exception a complex mix of good and bad, commendable and lamentable. Their every violent act was set in a complicated, multi-factional and political context that we can only begin to imagine from our seats of comfort over 100 years after the fact. And each violent act would have a nearly equal number of folks vociferously applauding it as condemning it. Because a shooting or hanging was done under the auspices of the law doesn't mean it was – or is – always just. Not by any means! But neither is a deadly ambush, without warning, in all cases an inappropriate of tactic!"

Simply said this is a good read. Author Jesse has a writing style which pulls the reader into the story and not only entertains but also educates. Read the truth about these eleven Old West Lawmen and enjoy real history.

Preface

Intensely Lived & Well Remembered Stories

by Jesse Wolf Hardin

My home lies in the the heart of the least populated county in the West, smack dab in the middle of the Gila wilderness of Southwest New Mexico. Among the many staunch individualists and rowdy opportunists who have either passed through these parts or called it their home, include the likes of the brilliant Apache war chief Geronimo and the classy yet deadly Billy The Kid. Butch Cassidy hung his Stetson at the WS Ranch down by the nearby village of Glenwood while laying low after his Colorado and Wyoming robberies. The Earp brothers rested up in the southern Gila's Silver City whenever they were on the run, and when the fiery eyed Elfego Baca held off a passel of murderous cowpokes he did so only a few miles from here. Within a short drive of my elk refuge cabin is the site of innumerable historic confrontations and shootouts over issues sometimes as insignificant as the draw of the cards or a drunk's unwise remark, other times in the course of unconscionable robberies, ambushes, and arrests. In some cases, all that was at stake was a cowboy's fragile manly pride, other times it was a person's liberty, a family's safety, or an entire way of life that was on the line.

Most often, when there is an argument or a violent contest, there will be two sides who feel sure that they are right. In civilized times and places, it is judges – partial or impartial – who are called upon to objectively decide the facts of the situation, what injustices may have been committed, and what resolution might be fair. In the West of old, it was more often to one's neighbors, village elders and heirloom firearms that a person would turn for clarity and redress. Even today, it takes an urban policemen so long to get to the site of an altercation, that he winds up doing a postmortem investigation rather than interceding in or preventing any conflicts or crimes, so you can imagine why folks often chose to take the law into their own hands in the sparsely populated parts of the historic West. And then as now, the region's lawmen could easily be biased or prejudiced, have a vested interest in own part or outcome or the other, fabricate and plant evidence in the interest of a hard to get conviction, or even be the ones actually perpetrating the robberies and shakedowns.

Lawmen, even the most amazing and courageous of them, tended to embody a mix of compassion and prejudice, generosity and avarice. None are the complete good guy heroes that we once read comic books about or idolized on the silver (or computer!) screen. Nor were even the worst of them likely to be totally bad as some revisionists insist. Like all human beings, they sometimes did things they shouldn't have, while other times gambling with their safety in order to save a stranger's life. It's only once we cease the lionizing and demonizing – the cynical sniping and blind worshipping – that we can look again at these fascinating personas from the 19th and 20th Centuries and see them for the incredibly complex individuals they were, people with common human traits and troubles doing extraordinary and occasionally incredible things with an undeniable intensity of character.

Whether known as sheriff, constable, marshall, deputy, ranger, policeman or peace officer, those who wore a badge found themselves caught between the demands of a city council or state government and the practical realities of hard-bitten frontier towns where freedom and opportunism were treasured and defended. Many received no pay other than a percentage of any money that those they arrested might be fined, contributing to the most honest officers having to moonlight at a second job, and others to turn to protection rackets or other crimes. Those who received salaries, usually made less than the not only the saloon-keepers but even the saloon sweepers, a monthly wage no better than that of the cowpunchers they rode herd on come Friday and Saturday nights. Their work could best be described as weeks of boring tasks, punctuated by moments of high drama and sometimes deadly confrontation. For these reasons and more, very few of even the most famous lawmen actually spent that many years wearing the star. While some like famed Jefferson Davis Milton could boast of lifelong lawman careers, they were the exceptions. Wild Bill Hickock, for example, served only a few stints between less officious gunslinging, while Wyatt Earp worked only as a policeman in a couple of Kansas towns and for less than 3 years, other than being temporarily deputized by his brother Virgil in time for the O.K. Corral gunfight.

The tales of most of the many thousands of hard working Western lawmen will never be recounted, and were never written down. For the following eleven stories, I've focused on both the well known and the little known, demythologizing some of the most famous and singing the praises of a few whose stories for various reasons, will never make it into the movies.

These stories are all the more compelling, however, because they are both true and unvarnished. At least, as true as I can determine! All events get a subjective slant from the very first recounting, the best a historian can do is dig deep and strive for balance, not sparing any criticism, while never failing to give them due understanding and credit.

The title "Lawmen of The Old West Unmasked" eludes to the wearing of masks by certain officers engaged in the commission of a crime, but more generally refers to the necessary "unmasking" of our chosen heroes as well as villains, revealing them as the compelling individuals they really are... impressive real life people, not comic book characters

The chapter on my homeboy Sheriff Elfego Baca also appears in a longer, gun-focused version in my book *Old Guns & Whispering Tales: Tales & Twists of The Old West*. Most of the others first appeared in the *Canadian Firearms Journal*, and it is largely thanks to the firing of their history loving editor that I switched my efforts from a column there to creating this book for you. I hope that it serves to not only inform you about times and deeds past, but also to inspire you in the now – kickstarting your imagination and putting your ideas to the test, getting you up and off of your favorite reading chairs and outside where you can act out your own valued missions and exciting adventures. And affirming your decision to keep an old shotgun in the closet or under the bed. The law can't help you, after all. They hardly ever could.

Opposing injustice and doing good is the job of every citizen even in a land with a zillion rules and laws, whether we work in law enforcement or take pride in being social outlaws. And it is not the timid, the self-doubting and retiring whose experiences and efforts will be remembered. It is the living of interesting, passion filled, highly driven lives that makes the tales of these eleven lawmen so memorable, and is that which can make our own lived stories worth retelling.

Every good lawman
started out a "little pistol" –
day-dreaming about growing up a
straight talker and straight shooter,
rescuing the beautiful heroine from the bad guys,
living a life that makes a good story.

Chapter I

Burton Mossman

The Good Captain Told The Governor Where To Stick It

It seemed the eyes of the murderous outlaw had never once left him... not in a whole night of the cowboy watching from the other side of a progressively dimming campfire for the dangerous desperado to drop his guard. Throughout the long hours, he strained to see beneath the bushy black eyebrows that had helped earn his quarry the nickname of *El Peludo*, the "hairy one." Now this *Peludo* leaned back against a saddle laid on the ground near the fire, just the same as the wary cowman did, with hands resting on a lap mere inches away from a sheathed but readied Colt. Burton Mossman had been introduced to Augustine Chacón only the night before by a pair of onetime deputies and full-time rustlers and train robbers. Now he pulled down on the brim of his hat and sat, motionless, as a bright display of stars paraded from one mountainous skyline to the other across an Arizona sky every bit as black as the charcoal at his feet once the embers had died out. Twice he was audience to courses of an extemporaneous coyote symphony, performed between long stretches of whispered desert winds and the barely discernible breathing of the *mal hombre* resting before him.

It was 1902, near the end of Mossman's one-year enlistment as Captain of the crime-busting Arizona Rangers. He was still upset about a petition that was circulating, calling for his resignation after he and a fellow ranger got into a public fistfight with a pair of deputies they believed were cheating at cards. An indignant Mossman had decided then and there that he would resign at the end of his enlistment... though not before capping off his brief but illustrious career with the recapture of this most notorious brigand in his own lair in Mexico, personally delivering him back to Solomonville, Arizona, and a noose with Chacón's name written on it. A flock of ravens could be heard croaking and cawing just as the stars began to give way to the first light of dawn, and he reasoned that his own burnished star would rise or fall with the morning's outcome. In less than an hour's time, he would either make a successful capture or feel the hot strikes of the gunman's .44 caliber slugs, his lifeless body sprawling unceremoniously on the sands, of consequence only to those coyotes and ravens hungry after their musical exertions.

While it was fairly unusual for a lawman to pose as a fellow criminal when affecting an arrest, it had long been common protocol to violate Mexico's sovereignty and penetrate far below the border whenever the authorities wished to reach out and touch a marauding band of Indians or extract a particular group of outlaws. Most often, this was accomplished by well planned kidnappings, either with or without the cooperation of Mexican *federales* with an equal disregard for the fine points and troublesome restraints of the law. Sometimes a nervy *puta* – a cantina prostitute – would be paid to drug the targeted miscreant's tequila, turning him over to some gringo deputy for a midnight ride back over the border and into a calaboose in the likes of El Paso, Silver City or Benson. Anyone – whether a Mexican national or U.S. citizen – who imagined they could commit crimes north of the line and then find safe refuge on the southern side, was just as likely to wake up one day to a cocked revolver being waved in their face, have a flour sack tied over their head, and their wrists lashed to the saddle horn of some sheriff or bounty hunter's horse.

This circumvention of the law by lawmen had the benefit of reducing the number of heinous perpetrators that escaped justice, but also played its part in a pattern of racial discrimination, land seizures, lynchings and summary executions committed in the border states from the 1840s until well after World War I. In one night in 1918, most of the male population of the little Texas village of Porvenir was shot down by an Anglo mob, and simply refusing to speak English could be seen as insubordination worthy of a beating. The last recorded "Old West" lynching of a Latino in the U.S. occurred in the not-so-old West in 1928, and it is a little known fact that as high a percentage of the Latino population was lynched in the border states as was the percentage of blacks in the deep South.

This explains why even the vicious *El Peludo* was held up as a Western Robin Hood by many of the Spanish speaking populous, as were a number of "brown skinned" outlaws from Southern Texas to Northern California... not because they had championed their people or been particularly generous with the poor, but simply because they had the temerity to strike out at an Anglo society that sought through legislation and intimidation to keep them

"in their place." No matter how venal the deeds of Augustine Chacón, his boldness served to temper the hearts of the Hispanics and bolster their often suffering self image. To his many admirers, the "Hairy One" was considered dashing as well as *muy macho* in his velvet pants and fitted vest, sitting boldly upright in the saddle even while riding through the leaden curtain of a posse fusillade. The giant bone-handled bowie knife tucked under his wide russet belt served as a tool of embellishment as much as intimidation, its tooled leather holster appropriately decorated with roses and hearts. Magnificence... *y corazon.*

None of this took away from the fact that Chacón was not only a remorseless but an utterly efficient and well practiced killer. Looking at the *Peludo* on that cold morn as he built up the fire, Burton Mossman most surely would have been remembering the stories he'd heard of the Mexican's prowess, verve and luck. It was widely said that he'd become an outlaw after being denied his cowman wages by a ranchman named Ben Ollney, and that a gunfight had ensured when Ollney made the mistake of laughing at his entreaties. When the smoke cleared, not only Chacón's employer but three of his pistoleros had perished in the thirty second gunfight. Mossman would also have heard about how his employer's brother had quickly raised a posse and surrounded the *bandito*, only to have him clench his reins with his teeth, fill both hands with revolvers, and then ride straight through the lawmen, killing four more as went. He'd have known that the entire Ollney family had been murdered in their home only two days later, and about the recent killing of yet four more men during the robbery of a mountain top saloon in Jerome, Arizona. Chacón didn't act out of sense of racial hatred so much as self preservation and enrichment, having no qualms about putting a rifle slug through the forehead of fellow Hispanic Pablo Salcido when the hapless deputy made the mistake of exposing himself under a flag of truce. Even more terrible, were the stories that housewives told over backyard fences and children whispered to each other by candlelight when they should have been asleep, tales of the several *Mexicano* sheep-shearers whose throats where found cut, and the dreadful rapes that the gang were alleged to have committed, every report and rumor undoubtedly contributing to this ultimate test of the Captain's nerve.

Just as troubling to him, must have been the knowledge that he couldn't be certain of getting Chacón from this patch of desert to his waiting coils of rope, even if he were able to capture his man alive. *El Peludo* had escaped from the Morenci jail back in 1895, almost as quickly as Graham County Sheriff Davis had deposited him there. And depending on the story, he had either dug through the ten inch thick adobe walls of the Tucson hoosegow in June of 1897, or else sawed his way through the bars on the window with a hacksaw blade smuggled to him in the spine of a Spanish bible. One of Chacón's many enamored lovers is said to have seduced the jailer in order to keep him deep in some other purpose, while some drunken mariachi singers in the next cell sang outlaw *corridos* to mask the noise of the escape. He'd remained a free man and successful rustler and robber for the last five years prior to the Captain getting on his trail.

The Scots-Irish blooded Burton C. Mossman, however, was no slouch either. His willingness to bet on himself in this intensely mortal game, was predicated on a proven record of ability, audacity and fortune that rivaled the *Peludo's* own. It had only been a little short of a year since Arizona Governor Nathan Murphy had tapped the well respected cowboy and onetime manager of the famous Hashknife outfit (the Aztec Land & Cattle Company) for a job as the first Captain of the reconstituted Arizona Rangers, a rough and rowdy unit chartered to rein-in the pervasive lawlessness in the remote southeastern corner of the state by any means necessary. In this role and mission, the enthusiastic 30 year-old outdoorsman had indeed excelled at a dangerous job, in tough times, in a region with a million places for an outlaw to hide.

That cattle rustling, train robberies and shootouts could still be so plentiful in the American Southwest at the turn of the "modern" 20th Century, might seem strange to many of you harkening from other, more civil parts of the continent. The confluence of Old Mexico, Southwestern Arizona and Southeastern New Mexico where I live, was still very much the "Wild West" at this late date, and remains so at least to some degree today. As described in my historical novel, *The Medicine Bear*, it is a land that has always attracted outliers and outcasts, as well as wild-eyed visionaries and committed independents. The freedom to carry a gun remains as core to its residents' beliefs today as it was for the past two hundred-plus years, and the remoteness of its towns and ranches results in an extreme degree of self reliance that extends into matters of medical care (often meaning the use of local medicinal herbs) and essential self protection.

The mystique-draped canyons and cliffside hideaways of The White, Mogollon and Burro Mountains, were allied with the drainages of the Salt, Blue, San Francisco and Gila Rivers in issuing a siren's call to raiders and outriders, from breakaway bands of renegade Apache warriors to gunslingers and bounty hunters. As I eluded to in the Introduction, the infamous Butch Cassidy and cohorts often wintered on the WS Ranch in the Mormon settlement of Alma, only 30 miles south of the cabin where I write this. My post office box is in the village once called Lower Frisco, where the Mexican-American Elfego Baca held off scores of attackers after making a ballsy citizen arrest. 150 miles from here, is the Mexican border and the tiny U.S. town of Columbus where a pissed-off Pancho Villa extracted vengeance for an American betrayal in

March of 1916, near where a single railway, the Southern Pacific, reported a dozen armed robberies between 1897 and 1900 alone.

The Arizona Rangers were reestablished in March of 1901, loosely modeled after the famed Texas Rangers. Their mandate from the governor was to put the damper on said illegalities and atrocities, in part to increase the chances of Arizona Territory finally being granted statehood. Mossman was made Captain to thirteen other men, each a genuine range rider chosen for his courage and savvy. They were required to supply their own rifle, handgun and horse, though they were allotted a decent wage and a small allowance to feed themselves and their mounts. Mossman's favorite arms included the ubiquitous Colt six-shooter, but also the more up to date Winchester 1895 rifle, with its box magazine allowing for the use of aerodynamic, pointed projectiles rather than the flat nosed bullets required for safe use in a tube-fed gun.

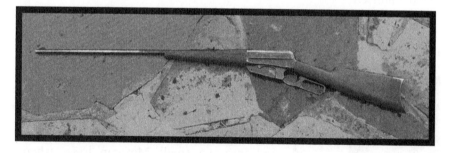

The flamboyant rangers were sometimes resented for getting all the limelight, or for being essentially the shock troops of a Republican governor in a region full of Democrats. But moreover, they were respected by the ranchers too long plagued with losses to thieves, lionized by the press, and applauded by readers from one coast to the next.

Almost immediately after being sworn in, Mossman and some of his men went after the notorious Wild Bill Smith gang, holed up on the Black River, losing both a ranger Carlos Tafolla and an Apache County deputy sheriff by the name of Bill Maxwell in the first awful fight. They succeeded in driving the gang over the border and out of the region for good, even though they never managed to actually catch Smith and company. That said, within a month they had also captured core members of the Musgrove gang, wanted for murder and theft in both Arizona and New Mexico, and within less than a year, the Captain and his rangers had nabbed 125 suspects, infiltrating the ranks of many of the local crime networks and outlaw gangs on what was known as the "Owlhoot Trail."

It was, in fact, disguise, infiltration and the use of informants that formed the strategy making possible the majority of Mossman's numerous accomplishments, with him sending out his men to work for various cattle outfits. Like a military tactician, he knew that the making of contacts, reconnoitering of the land and gathering of information could be the most important parts of the work, establishing the groundwork for accurate identifications, effective pursuits and surprise arrests. He was not, however, someone who led from behind the lines, and when it had come time to play the part of a horse thief in order to apprehend one of the most formidable of living outlaws, Burton would risk assigning no one but himself.

The Captain had received credible reports that two *Americano* robbers on the run in Mexico – the ex-lawmen Burt Alvord and Billy Stiles – were

Billy Stiles

wanting to come back home and try to "get clear"... and fortuitously, that they had lately taken up with the desperado he sought, Augustine Chacón. Wasting no time, Mossman rode totally alone over the border and into the small Mexican town where Alvord and Stiles were said to hang out, eliciting vague promises of help from them in exchange for a cut of any reward, and testifying on their behalf should they choose to return to the states to be tried. Then, on the prearranged day, he boldly rode into the camp shared by the Stiles, Alvord and the *Peludo*, the "Hairy One" Chacón.

Burt Alvord

There was no way that Mossman could be sure that either Stiles or Alvord wouldn't betray him in spite of their deal, or that they hadn't already "spilled the beans" already before he got there. Surviving the round of introductions, the Captain proposed that they join him in a raid to steal valuable racing horses from the Greene Ranch just over on the U.S. side. After asking a few questions, the wary Chacón sat down at the fire and pulled his oilskin drover's coat up around his neck just as a light drizzle of rain began to fall. Ominously, the Hairy One neither drank nor spoke throughout the remainder of the night, even as the rest of them shared a bottle of rye, talked and joked.

By first light, Alvord's anxiety over the betrayal was getting the best of him, and Chacón's suspicions were heightened further when Alvord nervously told them he was going to go look for water, riding out of camp with what proved to be no intention of coming back.

With that, Chacón finally spoke, saying he wasn't going any further with the proposed raid on Greene's, pulled out a Mexican cigarette, and struck a match on the heel of his boot. Sensing that he was running out of time, Mossman bummed one of the *cigarillos* from the fugitive and then squatted to light it with a faggot from the fire. At that moment, he dropped the flaming stick and drew his revolver from its leather in a single flawless motion.

"You're under arrest," he told him, leveling the fully cocked .44 at his furred and furrowed brow.

"Is this a joke?," the bandit is said to have blurted out, his eyes suddenly wide and flashing.

"It's no joke," Mossman then supposedly replied, before ordering Stiles to remove his gun and knife, and then to securely bind the perp's wrists for the ride north.

The tension on the trail must have been palatable, as they detoured around patrolling Mexican *federales*, with the Captain always riding behind the other two in case one or the other should try to pull something. Several times, in fact, Chacón threw himself off his horse and tried to run, until Mossman finally slipped a lasso around his neck, tightened it, and threatened to drag him over the border.

Once in the U.S. again, the retiring lawman flagged down a passing train headed for Benson. He was met at the station by Graham County Sheriff Page, arriving with a freshly made set of leg irons as well as steel handcuffs, and the two quickly agreed to the lie that Chacón had been seized on the U.S. side of the fence instead of illegally kidnapped from his home country of Mexico. The dapper, 46 year old brigand was then returned to Solomonville, where the gallows he'd cheated back in 1897 still awaited. Upon arrival, he was placed in a steel cage specially constructed for him, ensuring that this time there would be no escape from his morbid fate.

The hanging took place on "Black Friday," November 21st, 1903, behind 14' high adobe walls that blocked sight for all but the hundred or so citizens with official invites to the affair. I don't know if Mossman attended or not, but the crowd included 50 fervent friends and supporters as well as members of the Anglo community titillated by the spectacle of his death. The Hairy One had shaved off his beard in honor of the occasion, leaving only the heavy black mustache, and now walked up the gallow steps unassisted, with his head held high. Once at the top of the platform, Chacón asked for a cigarette and coffee, then launched into an eloquent half-hour long speech to those folks assembled before him in their best dresses and Sunday suits.

His final words to the celebratory townsfolk, mournful compatriots and tearful *señoritas*, were "It's too late now, time to hang." And just before the trapdoor was sprung, "*Adios, todos amigos!*" Both his admirers and detractors agreed on at least one thing: whether an unredeemable S.O.B. or icon of liberty, *El Peludo* was *muy bravo* to the very end.

There are unsubstantiated reports that the ex-ranger stuck around in Arizona just long enough to give character testimony on behalf of a rearrested Billy Stiles, before taking a much needed vacation in New York City at the invite of rancher Greene, the well-to-do owner of those targeted Spanish race horses. The Captain's commission had expired on the day of his return, and he already had plans made to return to the preferred work of ranching in his beloved New Mexico.

And we should note:

When the Governor offered him his badge back, the under-acknowledged Burton C. Mossman apparently told him exactly where to stick it.. a most unpleasant notion, I must say, given the renowned retentiveness of politicians, in juxtaposition with a star's characteristically jagged five points.

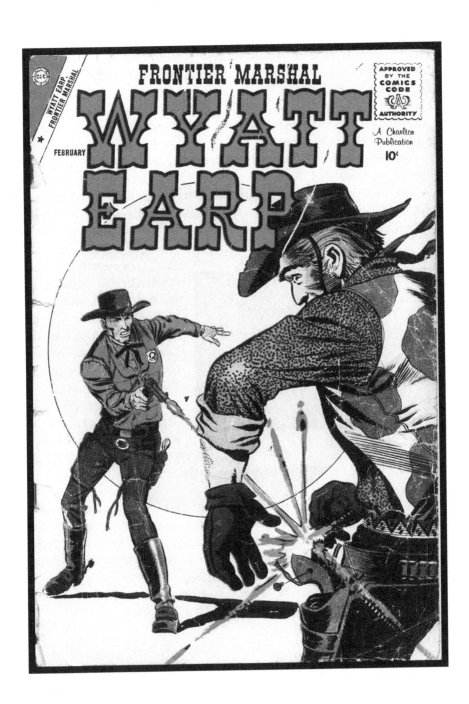

Wyatt Earp
1923

Chapter II

Wyatt Earp

As Crooked As He Was Courageous

"This is the West, sir. When the legend becomes fact, print the legend."
–from The Man Who Shot Liberty Valance, 1962

It is the image of Wyatt Earp and the O.K. Corral gunfight – or more accurately, the fight in a back alley near the O.K. Corral – that defines the western lawman for most people, as popularized by early sensationalist dime novel biographer Stuart Lake, featured in dozens of books in the years since, and burned into our memory thanks in part to the highly inaccurate movie Wyatt Earp and more so due to the powerfully acted but also fictionalized film Tombstone. We are comforted in this case, by the notion of a brace of officers standing up for law and order and protecting the innocents with an air knight-like nobility and fitting panache, unintentionally setting off a firefight with their well meaning enforcement of sensible gun control laws. Less comforting is the reality of two contending politicized factions of part time criminals and full time hustlers vying for control of the town of Tombstone, using an unpopular and seldom enforced ordinance against carrying guns as the excuse to confront a handful of cowboys who were already saddling up their horses and on their way out of town. There is something creepy about the Marshall pinning badges not only on Wyatt but on the colorful lawbreaker and killer Doc Holliday in order to carry out what many testified to be more of an execution than fair fight.

In the "days of yesteryear", and to some degree in these modern times as well, things like right, wrong, justice and law enforcement in the American West were anything but clear-cut. Instead of the proverbial black-hatted bad guys and white-hatted heroes, upon close inspection what we find are more like the gray hats of complex people acting on agendas that sometimes appeared – to certain vested interests, in specific situations – as being either dangerous threats to the community needing to be removed or else its brave defenders upon whom civilization itself seemed to depend. Not only were they judged differently depending upon the circumstances, but many at one time or other worked both sides of the fence.

While the job of lawman was always underpaid, it did provide potentially valuable inside information and special advantages sometimes contributing to officers branching out into extortion, or hanging up their badges altogether in exchange for a potentially more lucrative career of crime. Whether they were praised or reviled for their forays outside the law depended on the situation and context, and just who was doing the appraising. The bounty hunter Tom Horn was treasured by the well financed and often European cattle barons that hired him to both punish assumed rustlers and enforce their monopoly on grazing, but was hated by the small struggling homesteaders whom he primarily targeted. The respected lawman Sheriff Henry Brown of Caldwell, Kansas, was awarded a gold plated, presentation model Winchester rifle by a grateful citizenry for his services, but then took this same rifle with him on a botched robbery attempt on the bank in nearby Medicine Lodge.

At the same time, experience as a gunslinger and lawbreaker were excellent qualifications for the post of sheriff, and it often required bending or ignoring the fine points of law and order to get the job done.

In the cases of Hickock and the Earps, town managers were more than happy to overlook their zealous use of their Colt's revolvers to bludgeon or shoot the miscreants undeniably making life difficult for law abiding folk.

Wyatt Earp is a perfect case in point, our collective memory of him being one of a brooding anachronism with a flat brimmed hat and drooping mustache, a reluctant hero and near magician with a gun. More often and more accurately he was a gambler and provider of womanly flesh, a man whom many contemporaries referred to as the "fighting pimp". He can neither be wholly lionized, nor villainized, being more than anything typical of any of the "sporting men" who joined with the countless other opportunists who came west in search of riches and adventures. What distinguished him and others of his ilk, was a degree of hard-headed determination and a willingness to kill. But even given his various shooting scrapes, the primary reason we remember him is for the exaggerations and outright fabrications about his experiences that started with the release of those dime novels while he was still alive.

I grew up watching a fictionalized Wyatt Earp played Hugh O'Brien on TV, a morally spotless good guy always looking out for everybody but himself. To the contrary, the real Wyatt was in many ways a self serving and self aggrandizing scoundrel.

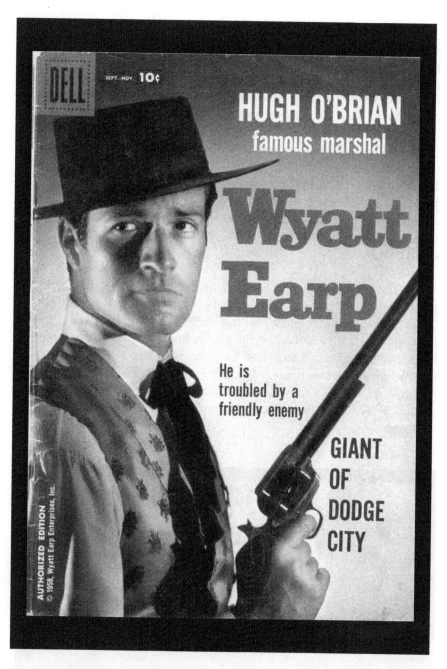

Wyatt was born March 19, 1848 to a family that locals came to call the "fighting Earps," since anytime the father and brothers weren't fighting other folks they could likely be found brawling amongst themselves.

When he got his first law enforcement job as constable of Lamar County, Missouri in 1870, he was heard to brag about how the badge made it possible to do as he liked without any more worry about being thrown in jail. A year later he had quit and moved on into the territory of the Cherokee, where he and a friend named Edward Kennedy were pursued, arrested and fined for rustling horses. By 1874 he could be found with his brothers Jim and Morgan and their mistresses in the then rowdy cow-town of Wichita, Kansas, where he made money gambling in the saloons and managing a stable of prostitutes... several of whom registered for business using the Earp last name. It was for kicks, it's said, that he joined local officers in tracking down a wanted miscreant, when the act of emptying their prisoner's pockets of $148 for "expenses incurred" reminded him of the extracurricular opportunities law enforcement work could provide.

Wyatt then got hired as a Wichita policeman himself in 1875, his performance described by the Wichita Weekly Beacon newspaper as "unexceptionable," the most exciting incident he was involved in being his dropping of his revolver on the saloon floor and being barely missed by his own bullet. Later that year he was arrested and fined for pummeling his boss's main rival during the election campaign for city Marshall. The Earps moved out of town two weeks after his dismissal, prompted by the city council issuing a warrant for their arrest as vagrants.

(Wyatt Earp Cap Pistol)

Wyatt Earp (seated) with
Sheriff Bat Masterson
Dodge City

Wyatt next worked two short stints as deputy of of Dodge City, possibly shooting one wanted man out the saddle during a chase, clubbing dozens of rowdy party-goers with the butt of his sixgun, and putting a bullet in the leg of a Texas cowpoke in the course of enforcing the ordnance against carrying guns in town. Resigning his post, he fatefully chose the silver mining town of Tombstone for his next attempts to strike it rich with as little effort as possible. It was there that he and his brothers came into conflict with an equally roguish band of part time rustlers who called themselves simply "the cowboys," with the Earps being both romanticized and provoked by the self proclaimed champion of "law and order", Tombstone Epitaph editor John Clum.

In March of 1881, the Benson stage was robbed by someone with insider information, and Wyatt came under suspicion. Years later his brother Virgil's wife wrote that she had hidden the masks and disguises they used, but regardless of the facts, things were heating up for what would be the shootout upon which much of Wyatt Earp's future fame will be predicated. In June, the then Mayor Clum appointed Virgil the town Marshall, who in turn temporarily deputized Wyatt and Morgan Earp as well as the always "game" Doc Holliday. By October 15th things had heated up between the contending parties and their respective political bases, beyond the point of hope for a peaceful resolution. It was ironic, many would agree, that the gun toting, often lawbreaking Earps would again use the enforcement of early, widely resented gun laws to spark the confrontation that everyone had been so long expecting.

On that infamous afternoon of October 26th, word had gone out that "cowboy" faction members Ike and Billy Clanton, Billy Clairborne and Tom and Frank McLaury were armed and gathered in the aforementioned alley, saddled and ready to ride out, though clearly making a point of taking their time. As was indicated by later trial evidence, of the five cowboys only Billy Clanton and Frank McLowry were "packing iron", while all three of the Earps and Holliday were carrying. While no hard documentation exists, it is reasonable to believe that each of the Earps carried ubiquitous Colt SAA revolvers in .45 or .44-40 caliber, the by far preferred handgun of the period, and that Holliday swung a double barreled shotgun in 10 or 12 gauge that Virgil had handed him, as well a Colt SAA and probably a backup Colt 1877 Lightning or Thunderer double action pistol as well. What Wyatt most certainly did not carry, was the extra long barreled, so called "Buntline Special".

The fight apparently went down much as dramatized in the movie "Tombstone," other than the ridiculous fanning of a dozen rounds into the nearby Fly Photography Studio: Virgil yells at the cowboys that "I want your guns," as Wyatt draws his Colt and Doc jabs his shotgun menacingly at Tom McLaury. The spunk Billy Clanton pulls his revolver in response, as an unarmed Tom McLaury struggles to get his Winchester 1873 rifle out of the scabbard on his horse. Somewheres up to 30 shots are fired in a space of around 25 seconds or so, a wild melee in which

Sheriff Behan pulls Billy Claiborne to safety, the troublemaking Ike Clanton runs, Billy Clanton shoots at Wyatt, Wyatt shoots at the more formidable Frank McLaury, and Earp exchange shots with Frank, and Doc putting two loads of buckshot into Tom as his horse spins out of his grasp. The fight ends with the thrice-shot and quickly bleeding-out teenager Billy Clanton hollering for more bullets as he clicked his emptied revolvers, and a dazed Morgan Earp and puckish Holliday now armed with a Colt handgun, facing down a wounded Frank McLaury who bravely asserts "I've got you now." "You're a daisy if you do," Holliday is reported to have replied, as he and Morgan simultaneously drop him dead. Scorecard: The McLaury brothers and Billy Clanton, deceased. Doc Holliday, a flesh wound to the hip. Morgan, a round in the shoulder. Sheriff Virgil Earp, a .45 caliber hole through is right calf. Wyatt, unscathed and movie-poster proud. Later, Wyatt and Doc are both arrested, and then freed in November. Judge Spicer felt obliged to drop charges in part because they hadn't gunned down the despised but unarmed and retreating Ike Clanton.

Dissatisfied with the ruling, cowboy compatriots ambushed and shotgunned Virgil Earp first, crippling him, and then blew away Morgan Earp as he bent over a billiard table. One of the suspected shooters was Frank Stillwell, who contrary to the movie version was at work at the stock yards in Tucson and not stalking the Earps when he first had his legs shot out from under him, and then suffered two loads of buckshot and four rifle rounds to the torso. Earp and friends put five holes in a second suspect, Indian Charley, before he could get away from the area, and the third suspect Pete Spence promptly asked Sheriff Behan to place him in protective custody. Satisfied at having taken the law into their own hands and extracted revenge, Wyatt and Doc left Arizona... but not as triumphant lawmen, as fugitives with warrants out for their arrest and a reward on their heads. For Earp, the O.K. Corral shootout was the historical high point from which he slowly spiraled down into a life of increasing irrelevance and personal desperation.

Hollywood actors aside, Wyatt never ever wore a badge again. Instead, in the ensuing years he travelled around the West with his brother Jim running confidence schemes and real estate scams, and were arrested a number of times including in Idaho on two counts of claim jumping. His notoriety won him honored work as referee of the world champion boxing match in 1896, a bout which he ended due to a foul he called against contender Fizsimmons, a judgment it was commonly believed was made because of bets Wyatt had placed on opponent Sharkey. As late as 1911, at age 63, Earp was arrested again for vagrancy and for bilking tourists in a bunco game.

(Wyatt Earp at right, while engaged in land fraud in Alaska)

In the end, it was no shootout that did him in. The year of the stock market crash, on January 3, 1929, Wyatt Earp died as he had lived: a "pain-in-the-arse"... not from bullet wounds, but from prostate cancer.

Wyatt spent much of his later period trying to get film star William S. Hart to publish his autobiography and make it into a movie, but Hart found problems with the manuscript's veracity. Stuart Lake held no such reservations, and printed his pack of colorful lies under the title "Wyatt Earp: Frontier Marshall." 70 years later there have been several imaginative programs and movies made about his life, with little understanding of or attention to the complexities and twists of this most famous lawman/outlaw. And we have what we has a collective people seem to need more than truth: the hope that can only come from an excitingly portrayed legend.

Chapter III

Harry Morse

Manos Arriba! – The Tireless California Manhunter

Harry N. Morse was at one point one the best known of all Western lawmen, far better known than Wyatt Earp during the years that they were both alive. Morse's portraits appeared regularly in newspapers all over the West, first for his exploits as the rifle wielding Sheriff, and later as a pioneering private detective trumpeted for such feats as helping to collar the infamous poetry reciting stage robber Black Bart. Harry's greatest fame and most exciting shootouts, however, came as a result of his lengthy and dogged pursuits of notorious Spanish-speaking desperadoes like Juan Soto and Tiburcio Vasquez, the kinds of men who had for decades been the terror of the incoming Anglo townsmen and entrepreneurs.

It is, of course, we writers of history who determine who is the terrorist, and who the terrorized... and like it or not, the most read histories are almost always those written by the victors and their descendants. While the fears of the Anglos were well founded, and a terrible number of heartless murders and robberies committed by brown skinned *Californios*, it should be noted that the innocents of their own community had also long lived in terror, though of the Anglo's whips and nooses, the many light skinned claim jumpers and plot squatters, the biased courts and their sometimes overzealous, sometimes ruthless enforcers. The once proud owners and inhabitants of Texas, New Mexico, Arizona and California were first colonized and then overrun by English speaking immigrants of primarily English, Irish and German ancestry, with the heaviest flood triggered by the California Gold Rush of 1848. Hispanic land claims were largely ignored, and their gold claims "jumped" by the greediest of the late arrivals. The effect on the earliest settlers was profound, and disturbing to say the least.

In 1856, Pablo de la Guerra made a powerful speech in front of the California legislature on behalf of the Hispanic population, "who have been sold like sheep by Mexico, who do not understand the language which is now spoken in their own country. They have no voice in this Senate. I have seen old men of sixty and seventy years of age weeping like children because they have been cast out of their ancestral homes. They have been humiliated and insulted. They have been refused the privilege of taking water from their own wells, and of cutting their own firewood."

The next big flood came near the outset of the Civil War, with the 1862 Homestead Act. The act was designed to parcel out large sections of "open land" while supposedly safeguarding existing land claims, but in reality few Hispanics had English speaking lawyers to represent them, the courts usually sided with the Anglos in any disputes, and ranches could be seized for not paying court costs resulting from any litigation. Anglo cowboys expected free rein with any young Hispanic women, but a man of Mexican blood who flirted with a "white" woman could be lashed with a rawhide bullwhip or dragged behind galloping horses through the cactus and brush. To the *bandidos* of these regions, robbery could be a way of getting back what they felt had either been stolen from them or denied them by virtue of their race. A relatively small percentage of the Hispanic population resisted, with most accepting their sad fates, so that those who did strike back stood out and became lionized folk heroes among their kind. Cutthroats from Joaquin Murietta to "Red Handed Dick" Procopio won the support of their communities through their defiance of the common enemy, and by the often dashing way in which these knights of plunder conducted their outlaw business.

It is common, of course, for criminals to justify their acts as righteous retribution, using their status as victims to rationalize their victimizing of others. In the 21st Century, religious and political extremists from the Moslem "holy warrior" Osama Bin Laden to the all-American Timothy McVey killed hundreds while playing the victim card. The Old West outlaw Jesse James, we must remember, was still robbing banks and dropping the hammer on Northern lawmen on behalf of the Southern cause long after the end of that unfortunate war between the states... and white settlers' militias once used "Indian atrocities" as the pretext for driving the entire native Sioux tribe from the rich Midwest farmlands that they coveted. Some of 19th Century California's so-called "social bandits" killed unarmed women and children as well as men, and a number preyed on their fellow Hispanics as well as the hated interlopers... but their greatest glory came from the fits they gave what had become the dominant system and society. To the English language newspapers, these outlaws were "greasers" and "brown devils" to be feared and when necessary, exterminated. To the desperadoes, it was Harry Morse who was the devil, the *gringo diablo* who hounded them in their own own hides and haunts, never letting up until he finally ran them out of the country or into the ground.

Hunting down suspects or escapees is usually only a small part of what a lawman does, though it fast became Harry Morse's stock and trade. It was his loyal Republicanism and reputation as a "take no guff" member of the Oakland Guardsmen militia that first got him elected Sheriff of Alameda County in 1864, close to the end of that awful internecine conflict absurdly christened the "Civil" War... but it was the skill he showed in pursuit of his adversaries that left an indelible impression on the public's imagination, fans and detractors alike.

In spite of a proven ability to knock his enemies out with a single punch, at 5' 7" and 155 pounds, Morse was anything but an imposing specimen, and at the time he pinned on his badge he was still (in his own words) "as green in the business as a man can be." He barely knew how to use a gun, and couldn't even speak the language of a large swath of the population. His first two years in office were in fact utterly unremarkable, notable only for the paucity of lawbreakers residing in his jail, as Harry slowly but methodically and painstakingly went about learning what he believed he needed to know to become the most effective and feared manhunter in the entire territory. First on his agenda was learning to speak Spanish, so that he could communicate with the network of local informants who would prove again and again to be one of his greatest advantages. He worked to become expert on horseback, in preparation for the fast chases and plodding marathon rides that lay before him. He would, after all, be gone from his family for up to five weeks at a time, to the disappointment of his wife Virginia. Tracking skills were high on his "git-to" list as well, and it wasn't long before he was able to discern the number of horses on a trail, whether they were being ridden or not, if they were uniformly shod and even their physical condition, including whether they favored a certain foot. Last but not least, Harry Morse practiced shooting at both sitting and moving targets, at a variety of ranges, after arming himself with some of the best firearms of his day.

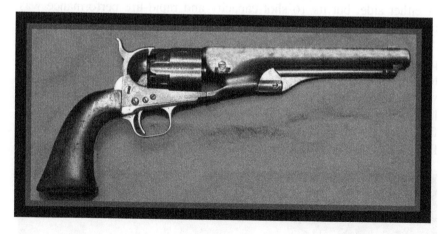

When it came to handguns, he joined with a majority of Westerners in laying his money down for Colt's revolvers, both a powerful .44 cap and ball Army model, and a much smaller 1849 Pocket model.

It was his long guns that he counted on the most, however. His first choice in any altercation, starting with the tactical rifle of the day, was the prototype for future Winchesters: the tube fed Henry. Introduced in 1860 at the onset of the war, it saw only limited service with the soldiers of either side, but its 16 shot capacity and rapid-fire performance was impressive enough to earn it the affections of the men, and the title of "the gun you can load on Sunday and shoot all week." The Henry proved devastating during Red Cloud's War in 1866, when lever and toggle actioned Henrys in the hands of a few miners were used to kill or wound up to 60 attacking Sioux. The warriors were expecting the usual lengthy reloading time of the conventional single shot muzzle loading firearm, and were thoroughly surprised by the fast repeat shots emanating from what was one of this period's true technological marvels.

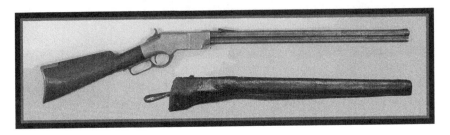

However, as effective as it was at distances of 80 yards or less, it was no way near the "deadly at 1,000 yards" rifle that was claimed in many a magazine article. The cartridge's 26 to 28 grains of black powder pushed the .446" diameter, 200 or 216 grain bullets out of its 29" barrel at only 1,125 feet per second, producing a modest 568 foot pounds of muzzle energy, roughly the ballistics of a standard modern .45 ACP round fired out of a short barreled handgun.

The Henry-toting Morse was reelected in September of 1865, by the same Republican majority. His early failures inspired rather than discouraged Morse, after which he "commenced to gather them in," as he put it. Harry's first success at manhunting came the following year, with the pursuit and arrest of fugitive cattle rustler Eduardo Gallego, and his first gunfight soon after. He would engage with his Colt, however, and not with his rifle which he'd foolishly left in its scabbard on his stationed horse. He bore nothing but his holstered revolver as he waited on foot in the shadows of a backroads cantina, for the noted robber and gunslinger Narciso Bojorques.

Bojorques was both widely feared, and widely admired. His waylaying and "winging" of Bay Area meat cutter John Gunnell had been the final straw for Sheriff Morse, whom Narciso had long bragged would never catch him – and who he said would surely die if he ever tried. Warned by an informant that the bandito could be arriving at the remote cantina anytime, the sheriff had a pretty good idea it was him when he did indeed approach in the pitch darkness, hooves clopping in the proud way of Spanish trained horses, and an attendant jangling of vaquero's spurs. Morse stepped out of the shadows just as Bojorques rode towards the small circle of light cast by the eatery's oil lamps, but his quarry backed away a split second before he could grab the reins, simultaneously pulling a gun and pointing it in the general direction of a threat he had not yet fully assessed. "No poder, señor," he said, "it can't be done," as Morse fumbled for his still sheathed Colt, any moment expecting to hear or feel a ball exploding in his direction. Fortunately for him, the bandito continued to waver undecided for the second or two the lawman needed to finally jerk his revolver free and snap off a barely aimed shot, smashing into the elbow of a rider once again made nearly invisible by the black folds of night.

Bojorques spun about on his mount, racing off towards the hills until running against a rail fence. Morse fired four more times at the dimly outlined figure, before he managed to get his horse to leap the fence and carry him safely away. The fugitive would be killed the following year, meeting his demise not in a failed arrest or stealthily laid ambuscade, but instead engaged in an honorable duel with an Arizona cowboy over a disputed hand of poker.

One by one the area's most wanted men were "nipped" by the determined Morse, as he made it his cause to run down every lawbreaker that came to his attention. With there being no state police agency, he became the de facto hired gun, enlisted by other counties and jurisdictions to help terminate the most difficult cases. One by one he laid his traps, all across northern and central California, bringing what had once been an empty jail up to full occupancy. And for a second time, Morse lost a man he'd shot and wounded, when in in October of 1867, he ambushed Narato Ponce, exchanging fire with the wanted murderer before shooting the escaping culprit in the back, and then losing sight of the badly wounded hombre in the concealing dark. Oakland Daily News reports crowed that their sheriff was "on the warpath," and that "if any man can secure the criminal, Harry is the man." This "securing" was more than once accomplished by Morse manipulating evidence and perjuring himself before a court of law, such as when he lied to win a conviction of indisputable bad guy Procopio Bustamonte. He bent the law he was sworn to uphold, not out of a sense of vengeance like Wyatt Earp did. As much as loved the cash rewards, when he committed injustices it always out of the sense that he was doing the right thing, assuring himself he was making the community safer by helping to send one man after another to the state penitentiary.

Morse's next big feature in the papers came when he set out to take down the notorious Juan Soto, described by his friend Sheriff Nick Harris as "a perfect type of desperado, over six feet high, well proportioned, and quick as a cat, with a countenance the worst I ever saw in a human face." That said, many an amorous young señorita considered him plenty attractive, and it was while visiting a casita known for its womenfolk that he was uncovered by Harry Morse and San Jose policeman Theodore "Sam" Winchell.

Soto was known for his fancy dress, velvet shirts worn over concho studded breeches that tucked into squared toed, knee high muleskin boots. Over this outfit he wore a long blue Union Officer's coat, with a finely woven blanket tied to his shoulders like a rakish cape, a heavy cartridge belt girdling beneath it with a brace of ivory handled .44s. Unlike many of his contemporaries, however, his fine dress belied his despicable manners. This was driven home by his needless shooting of the unarmed clerk of the Thomas Scott Store on January 10th, 1871, planting a slug in the Italian immigrant's chest as he kindly held the door open for him to enter the establishment.

It was the following year that Morse got word of Soto dallying with certain ladies, and closed in on what would become the site of his next gunfight. The lawmen obviously expected Soto to be nearby as they approached the aforementioned casita, yet still claimed to have been surprised to find him seated there at the table as two of the officers entered the room. Sheriff Morse drew and cocked his single-action revolver, while commanding *"Manos arriba!"* – "Hands up!" Rather than complying, the fugitive simply sat and stared at his much loathed enemy, refusing to

move. "Put these on him," Morse hollered at Winchell, tossing him the handcuffs. Like Soto, Winchell remained motionless at the order, although frozen in fear rather than braced by contempt. A few long seconds of silence passed, until constable Winchell could stand it no more and burst back out the door. "No tira en las casa!" – "Don't shoot in the house! – the hostess begged, grabbing hold of the sheriff's shooting arm, as Morse shoved aside the woman he'd later refer to as "a Mexican Amazon" then backpedaled out the same door Winchell had just exited.

Bloodthirsty outlaw Juan Soto responded to Sheriff Harry Morse's commands not by running away, but by getting up from the table and chasing both of the offending lawmen out the door. Witnesses later described how the bandito fired his pistol from the hip as he advanced, with Morse falling to the ground after each shot as though hit. As many as four times in a row, Soto blasted away and Morse hit the dirt, each occasion jumping right up again and returning fire. But was Morse's last shot that was the first to make contact, smashing Soto's pistol at the breech and driving it upwards into his face. Soto then made a run to escape across an open field, as Harry rushed to his horse and unsheathed his prized new rifle.

Shining in the morning sun, was the polished brass frame of the Henry's successor, the Model 1866 Winchester nicknamed the "Yellowboy" by its ardent fans. This particular example – serial number 13727 – was inscribed "Harry N. Morse, Sheriff Alameda Co.," as befitting its acclaimed owner. All 1866s featured a revised action and easy to grip wooden forearm. With efficient lever loading and a high capacity tubular magazine similar to the Henry, the Model '66 garnered an immediate following on the strife torn frontier.

150 yards is a very long ways for the slow moving .44 rimfire round, but it was at this extended range that Harry is reported to have connected with his first round from the flashy new carbine, the lead slug piercing Soto's left shoulder and readily convincing him of the impossibility of getting away. Once more, Juan's unfailing instincts were to attack his tormentors. Pulling revolvers with both hands, he quickly strode towards the gathered lawmen, yelling and firing as he approached. Subsequent shots from sheriffs Morse and Harris failed to find their mark until, still some 70 yards from his goal, a second round from Harry's '66 took the top of Juan Soto's head off, effectively and dramatically ending the fight.

The odds of Morse hitting a moving man that far away with what is basically a pistol-powered round, makes it one of the more phenomenal shots fired in Western gunfight history. It is reminiscent of buffalo hunter Billy Dixon's 1874 killing of a Comanche war chief at nearly 9/10ths of a mile, using a heavy barreled Sharps in "Big" .50/90 caliber... both feats being damn unlikely, mighty lucky, and memorable as hell.

Less extraordinary, was Morse's subsequent framing of the man he believed had been an accomplice to Juan Soto's murder of the Scott's Store clerk, an Hispanic who just happened to be innocent of the charges he was so wrongly convicted of. Bartolo Sepulveda had the misfortune of being Hispanic, being an amigo of Juan's, and most importantly, appearing with him at the scene of the crime only a day before it occurred. Never mind that so many witnesses stepped forward to swear that Sepulveda was elsewhere at the time of the murder, the sheriff was convinced he was involved and would do whatever was necessary to see him behind bars.

For two years, Morse hounded Sepulveda, preventing him from rendezvousing with his family or keeping a job, always close but never quite closing with his quarry. Then on March 20th of 1873, an unarmed Sepulveda surprised Morse by walking into his office and surrendering to him. Bartolo could just as easily stepped through the door and executed this man who had been making his life so miserable, but this fact did nothing to dampen Morse's zeal to put him away. The sheriff once again committed perjury to ensure the outcome, and went a step further this time, arranging for the pardon of a convict, John Copp in exchange for his claiming he'd heard Sepulveda confess to the murder when they shared a cell. Bartolo Sepulveda suffered twelve awful years of imprisonment before the bribery and set up were revealed, and Morse's innocent victim was finally released in 1885. Bartola reunited with his wife and children and lived the life of a rancher without any further run-ins with the law, until saddening his many friends, children and grandchildren by dying of old age in 1926.

Harry resigned as Sheriff of Alameda County at the beginning of 1878, after squabbling over wages and expenses. He had served in that position for an amazing 14 years during which the county population and tripled, but the result was that there was no longer the heavy Republican majority needed to keep him in office. While he was quoted as saying money was never the motivation for his pursuits, it was clear that he had tried for and won many a cash reward, so much so that he was able to make a number of investments including the purchase of a sawmill. With his pride intact and money in the bank, Harry went on to form and direct the Morse Detective Agency, one of the first of its kind in the western U.S. There would be one more dramatic manhunt before that, however, in which he'd ride over much of the state in search of yet another "scourge of all civilized peoples" and "hero of his people."

Tiburcio Vasquez was another robber who took special pleasure in lashing out against the *Norte Americanos*, the white skinned Anglo-Saxons known for discriminating and misusing those born of Spanish and Mexican descent. While only 5' 5" tall, he felt his wit and actions large enough to help precipitate the return of California to Mexico, though three different times they had resulted in his imprisonment in San Quentin instead. He formed his own gang at an early age, and by 1856 Vasquez was known from Sonoma County to the San Joaquin Valley as a particularly dangerous holdup artist, horse thief, cattle rustler and stage robber. His cohorts during this time included other Morse targets Procopio ("Red-Handed Dick") and Juan Soto. It was a bloody robbery in August of 1873, that resulted in the governor placing a $1,000 on Vasquez, "Dead or Alive," inspiring as many a dozen posses including Sheriff Morse's to hit the trail in search of him and his men. Pressure from Morse and the others made his familiar Northern California haunts just a mite too hot for him, and he soon moved his robbing and pillaging operations south.

Sometime in 1874, Vasquez came in from his outlaw camps in the San Gabriel Valley and moved into a cabin owned by Syrian native Georgias "Greek George" Caralambo, on Rancho La Brea land in the still undeveloped hills of what later became the crowded city of West Hollywood. George had retired to ranching after a stint as one of the few U.S. Army camel drivers during the failed experiment to set up a dromedary supply line across the harsh deserts of the Southwest, and now a lady friend of his wife's had attracted Tiburcio's attentions.

In the interest of protecting this young woman's virtue, her family was more than willing to tell Morse all they knew. Knowing full well that he was working outside his jurisdiction, Morse shared his information with the Los Angeles sheriff, Billy Rowland. Rowland told Morse that the information was wrong and his source unreliable, sending him away disappointed. And yet oddly enough, it wasn't long after Harry's departure that Rowland sent his own deputies to surround Creek George's cabin. Vasquez leaped out of a window and began running when he spotted the lawmen, but was shot in his back like a good many of his kind. Tiburcio survived, only to be hauled wounded and bleeding to the L.A. caboose.

Sheriff Morse had logged 2,720 horseback miles searching all over Central and Southern California, and now without the reward he would have to bear all the expenses himself. He nonetheless made the trip back to see Vasquez hung in 1875. Harry was standing next to him on the platform as he said his goodbyes to the many friends and smitten women who stood crying in the assembled crowd. "Pronto, Pronto!" were his final words, in a brave show of disregard for death. Apart from all the ways he was demonized by the new dominant culture, Tiburcio Vasquez was still nothing less than a ruthless, professional killer. And yet, one only need read some California history written from the Hispanic perspective, to get a completely different view of this infamous bandito. I'll share just a single anecdote, referenced in a 1956 article by Rodney Johnson that I dug up during my research:

German-born "Cattle King" Henry Miller was one of the largest land holders of the 19th Century, half owner of 1.4 million acres of California grazing and farm land, with grazing rights on another 22,000 square miles worth. Sometime in the early 1870s, he was held up by four masked men on the Pacheco Pass trail. As he handed over his money, Miller pointed out that he now had no funds to complete his trip. Appreciating the situation, the leader of the gang took a couple of gold coins out of his bag and handed them to the Cattle King, remarking *"No problemo...* pay me back the next time you see me!"

Miller was sitting in a finely appointed San Luis Obispo hotel lobby a few months later, when he thought he heard the same robber's voice in the next room over. Stepping up to the mahogany bar where Vasquez stood, he shook his hand and handed him $20. "Here's the money I owe," the cool Miller told him, "and thank you very much for the use of it." Vasquez reacted

with an often unreported degree of outlaw élan, buying him a drink, and then ever after warning his cohorts neither harm nor harass "the man who always pays his debts."

In my lifetime, there has been a huge controversy and public outcry every time a street or public building is named after the murderous but in some cases chivalrous champion of the dispossessed, including an elementary school in Salinas, California, and a medical center in Hayward. Families who have suffered their own discriminations, with offspring who like Bartolo Sepulveda have sometimes been railroaded in the courts, still think harshly of Morse, his vendetta and techniques, and find inspiration in the lifelong rebelliousness of these bandito forebears.

Morse remains a hero, nonetheless, to the Anglos – and even some of the more conservative Hispanics – of the state of California. When he died of natural causes in 1927, there were some of both in attendance at his funeral. Discussions about his prejudices and excesses continue to this day, but none contest that he was one of the most irrepressible, diligent and effective manhunters ever.

Chapter IV

Bucky O'Neill

Arizona's "Most Many-Sided" Man

"Dauntless courage and boundless ambition..."
–President Theodore Roosevelt

Engineer Charlie Wood peered intently through the locomotive windshield and swirling flakes of snow, illuminated in the lampblack night by the lanterns on the front of his Santa Fe Eastbound #2. A heavy sheep lined jacket and leather workman's gloves kept him warm as he worked the frigid steel throttle of the coal-stoked engine and watched for the dim amber lights marking the small Canyon Diablo Station. Unbeknownst to him, only a short ways ahead four other gloved men squatted over a tiny campfire, weathered cowboy hats set low and the collars of waxed canvas drover's coats pulled high to help protect them from northeastern Arizona's Winter winds. Ghost-white steam vented from the sides of the engine as Charlie slowly pulled the train to a stop in front of the station office and elevated water tank. From the lip of a jacket pocket hung a cast brass fob in the shape of a longhorn steer's head, and it was this he used to easier pull out the hunter-cased railroader's pocket watch and note the precise arrival time: 1:00 AM exactly. March 20th, 1889.

The station was built near the rim of Diablo Canyon and the iron trestle bridge that bore the Santa Fe's tracks from its northern to southern side, and adjacent to the ruins of what had before the bridge's completion been a briefly bustling if entirely notorious "settlement of sin." Newspapers of the time called Canyon Diablo the "toughest Hellhole in the West" and the "West's deadliest town." From the time of its founding as a railroad construction camp in 1880, it seemed a strong magnet for gamblers, prostitutes and fugitives giving a wide berth to the law-drenched cities of Tucson and Phoenix. It's residents were fairly resistant to civilizing, it could be said, given that Canyon Diablo's very first town marshal was in the hands of a coroner by 8 o'clock, after having just been sworn that day at 3. Seven marshals in 14 months either hit the trail or bit the dust, until the bridge work ended and demolition began in 1882.

Wood's young fireman opened the cab door, grabbed the ladder rail and eased himself down the steps to the ground. The punctual engineer soon followed, and was barely turned around when two men wearing frightening flour-sack masks stepped out the blackness with revolvers drawn and his fireman in tow. "Hands up!" was the cliche demand and yet one easily understood and perhaps wisely followed, as the two fired some shots into the air and through the wall of the office as audible exclamation points. The robbers quickly shoved them over to in front of the Express Car carrying the mail and safe, inside of which stood company messenger E. G. Knickerbocker holding a shortened Remington double-barreled shotgun in his trembling hands. He could hear the shouts to "Open up!", but only when the fireman yelled out that the outlaws had dynamite and would blow the car up, did the wary Knickerbocker set aside his trusty 12 gauge and slide wide the weighty metal door.

The two bandits, later identified as Dan Harvick and J.J. Smith, climbed in and began threatening the messenger to get him to open the main safe, a slight man who nonetheless bravely convinced them that it had a time lock and could not be opened. Knocking him aside, they instead looted the Wells Fargo box of its stash of  jewelry and cash. Leaping out and firing a few more rounds to discourage any possible do-gooder hero types from getting in the way, they ran to rejoin their compadres Bill Sterrin (or Steiner) and John Halvard (or Halford), each holding the reins of two horses in one hand, while providing cover with the Colt .44s in the other. So dark was the night, that were out of sight in a flash, only the soft sound of galloping hooves reporting back on their fast paced escape.

The four men stopped only a few miles distant, built a second small fire and sorted through their loot. Later reports of the Santa Fe Railroad's losses varied anywheres from $1,500 to $35,000. The company was said to inflate the amount taken in robberies at times in order to qualify for a larger insurance payment, and most certainly underreported the takes on other occasions, to both reduce their embarrassment and the heat from stockholders. Whatever the actual figure, it was a none-too-shabby wage for cowpokes accustomed to earning $30 a month. Flushed with their success, we can easily imagine them making jokes about the look of surprise on the wide-eyed engineer's face, or how much a man could accomplish with a stick of TNT without ever having to light it. If so, it was in part thanks to a certain level of obliviousness: Oblivious that the Arizona Territorial Legislature had only a month earlier passed a bill making train robbery punishable by death. Clueless that their burglary of supplies from the Barnes Ranch right before the robbery meant they had owner Will Barnes and his buddy Billy Broadbent already hard on their trail. And unaware that they were to be dogged and treed by one of the more interesting – and determined – lawman in the state's history, the chain smoking, soft talking William Owens "Bucky" O'Neill.

"If you done it, it ain't bragging."
–Walt Whitman

O'Neill was born on February 2, 1860 – most likely in St. Louis – to a father cited for heroism while fighting with the Irish Brigade during the War Between The States. He moved to Phoenix, Arizona and away from his family in the Fall of 1879, following his graduation from college in Washington, D.C. at age 19. It was while working as a typesetter for the *Phoenix Herald* newspaper that this lover of Walt Whitman's sensual nature poetry – this ever so gentle and considered man – earned the not so soft-sounding nickname of "Bucky"... not for any reputed prowess over bucking stallions, but for his enthusiastic and unrestrained bets while regularly "bucking the tiger" at backroom faro games. It was also in Phoenix that he underwent the proverbial "baptism by fire," shortly following his appointment as a special deputy to Marshall Henry Garfias.

Three drunken cowboys caught the lawmen's attention by riding up and down Washington Street target practicing on the mercantile signs swinging in front of the drinking establishments and shops. The nerviest or craziest of these celebratory hombres, Bill Hardy, rode his horse through the swinging doors of the Tiger Saloon to order up a drink, but bumped his head on a chandelier and shot the ceiling full of holes instead. The sheriff was heard to holler for them to "hold up" just as he rejoined his friends mounted in the middle of the street, but their trusted counsel, whiskey, apparently advised them to charge with guns blazing. The sheriff and his new deputy chose to stand their ground and return fire, and depending on the account, it was either Garfias or O'Neill who neatly drilled the lead rider, effectively ending both the party and the fight.

For whatever reasons, Phoenix didn't "shine" for Bucky, at least not as brightly as the silver bullion and faro tables of the then new boomtown of Tombstone, where he briefly worked for John Clum's *Tombstone Epitaph*, or the mining-rich capital city of Arizona Territory, Prescott, which drew him to its bosom in the Spring of 1882 and remained his home for the remainder of his life.

O'Neill volunteered for the Arizona Grays militia, worked as court reporter, wrote for the newspaper *Arizona Miner*, launched his own periodical for cattlemen he called *The Hoof and Horn* in 1885, and got married to Pauline Schindler the same year. He then ran successfully for Yavapai County probate judge and superintendent of schools, focusing much of his time to improving the rates of literacy in preparation for the Territory's bid for U.S. statehood. It was while a judge that he once happened upon a small group of Navajo sheep herders being denied access to a watering hole by some rowdy railroad workers, and in rather unjudgely fashion, rode hard towards the miscreants and cleared the way for the hapless Navajo and their dying of thirst herd.

Always ready for new experiences and challenges, in 1888 the ever more popular Bucky gave up his judgeship in order to run for sheriff of Yavapai County on the Republican ticket. He inspired both the support of most of the county's residents and the active opposition of railroad officials, by pledging to assess the railroad the full value of its land holdings if elected. Railroad officials did everything they could to prevent his being chosen, making it even more admirable that he would undertake a manhunt a year later on their behalf.

"There is no week nor day nor hour when tyranny may not enter upon this country, if the people lose their roughness and spirit of defiance."
–Walt Whitman

In spite of the Santa Fe Railroad executives downplaying the significance of the Diablo Canyon train robbery, a reward of disputed size was posted, and the intrepid Bucky O'Neill immediately set out to bring about the perpetrators' capture. Riding with deputies Ed St. Clair and Jim Black, plus Santa Fe detective Carl Holton, the posse met Barnes and Broadbent on the trail and took their place on the robbers' trail. The desperados ahead had tried every trick in the book to throw off the expected pursuit, from riding along creek bottoms and moving with wild horse herds, to wrapping their hooves with burlap as they zig-zagged north into Utah, but still their pursuers remained true.

In the photograph of the four posse-men, we can see that Sheriff O'Neill and his deputies all pack the archetypal Colt single-action revolver on their hips, while the detective has a "modern" double-action Colt 1878 . 44 holstered at his side. Everyone holds a toggle-link action Winchester 1873 rifle in the .44WCF handgun cartridge... except for Bucky, who we see grips the barrel of a much improved, John Browning designed Winchester Model 1886, firing a full power rifle load.

It was with this Winchester, that Bucky got things rolling when they finally cornered the Diablo gang At Wahweep Canyon, the bandits seeing they were boxed in and attempting to charge right through the approaching posse. Smith's white horse goes down with O'Neill's first shot, and then Bucky's own gelding is hit between the eyes and collapsed underneath him. Soon all are afoot, Halvard and Sterrin throwing their guns

down and their hands up, and Smith and Harvick leaping down the cliffside. Several miles later, Bucky spots the two men prostrate and drinking from a water hole, preempting possible resistance by sending a round splattering into the rock they lay belly down on.

He had his quarry fully corralled now, and without anyone being hit on either side of the brief gunfight. The Railroad reluctantly paid the reward, split four ways among the officers, but refused to reimburse Sheriff O'Neill for his expenses on the trail. Their excuse, legitimized by a court of law, was that Bucky had left the county without permission when chasing the Diablo gang all the way into Utah!

The corporations may not have liked him, but the common man voted him into one office after the other. As soon as his term as sheriff was up, O'Neill ran for and was elected unanimously to be the Mayor of Prescott.

And disgusted with the traditional political parties including his once beloved Republicans, he came close to winning a United States Representative seat as a member of the upstart agrarian, egalitarian and libertarian Populist Party.

When the Spanish-American War broke out he had been living a quiet and somewhat uneventful life. When Teddy Roosevelt's regiment was being formed, nearly 300 cowboys, miners, citizens and politicians joined with him and they rode to San Antonio, Texas and were received with open arms. This group became Troop A, 1st United States Volunteer Cavalry (Rough Riders).

> *"Nothing endures but personal qualities."*
> −Walt Whitman

In April of 1898, the United States declared war on Spain over numerous issues including their ownership of Cuba, just off the coast of state of Florida. An explosion on the U.S. warship Maine was blamed on sabotage, though was later determined to have been an accidental coal gas explosion, when the hull was found to have been blown outwards and not inwards as would be the case with a mine. "Remember the Maine" nonetheless became the motto that aroused the American citizenry to rally behind an invasion of the island, not unlike the American invasion of Vietnam being predicated on a torpedo attack on a U.S. ship by the North Vietnamese that all evidence indicates never happened. Pretext or pretense was not first on the mind of Bucky O'Neill, however, when he was one of the very first to answer Theodore Roosevelt's call for a force of volunteers made up of the kinds of resourceful and rough-hewn Westerners and able horsemen that he so respected, cowboys and trackers, sharp shooters and lawmen. And so too, he attracted the lawbreakers, Western outlaws anxious for a way to avoid stateside authorities while acting on their patriotic instincts and eagerness for adventure.

The first volunteer mustered into the army for the war with Spain was the then 39 year old William Owens O'Neill, entering as a private but quickly being promoted to Captain of the Rough Riders' Troop A. Promoted to serve as one of his sergeants, was the same robber, Bill Sterrin, that he'd exchanged shots with in Utah, free after nine years in the state penitentiary and, having enlisted under an assumed name and apparently proud to be serving under the onetime lawdog who had run him aground.

We get a glimpse of the prevailing cavalier attitude of the Rough Riders in the dinner toast made on the boat trip over, as all in the galley raised their wine glasses high: "May the war last long enough for every officer to be either be killed, wounded or promoted!"

When the volunteers got to Cuba, they were disappointed to hear that there had been no transportation provided for their prized horses and that they would be fighting on foot, but they remained no less anxious for action and a chance at glory. One of their objectives was to silence a fortified bunker positioned near but not on San Juan Hill, a long climb up an exposed slope through a what they called a "blizzard" of hot steel and lead. Roosevelt had bought many of them Model 1895 Winchesters out of his own pocket, another Browning designed lever action repeating rifle featuring a novel box magazine instead of tubular, allowing for the first time the safe use of ballistically superior pointed bullets. And unlike the Buffalo Soldiers who were issued older single shot trapdoor Springfields firing black powder cartridges, the 1895 Winchesters and Norwegian made, bolt-action Krag-Jorgensen rifles both fired the smokeless .30 U.S. (.30/40 Krag) round. The billowing puffs of white smoke from the black men's Springfields made them easy targets for the Spaniards with their modern Mauser rifles, while the Rough Riding infantry carried certain equals. Machine gunners on both sides spit out their own torrents, adding to the terror and tumult, ripping through flesh that thinned the ranks of the cowboys as well as the white suited Hispanics.

Temporarily hunkered down in a slight depression, Captain O'Neill paced back and forth before his men, defying death to demonstrate an example of bravery worthy of following, alternately shouting encouragement and Whitman quotes to what must have been his incredulous as well as wholly impressed bronc tamers and Indian fighters. It was the heat of July, and some of them were weakened and shaking from Malaria delivered by that humid country's countless mosquitos, but all believe in the potential of their own efforts if not only the sanity of the cause. And all seemed to believe in and respect the nerve of their commander.

"Get down, Captain, or you'll be killed for sure!" a concerned Sterrin was heard to implore.

O'Neill took his cigarette out of his mouth, as Roosevelt would later recount, "and blowing out a cloud of smoke he laughed and said, 'Sergeant, the Spanish bullet isn't moulded that will kill me.' A little later... as he turned on his heel, a Spanish bullet struck him in the mouth and came out at the back of his head, missing his teeth; so that even before he fell, his wild and gallant soul had gone out into the darkness."

"O'Neill is the most many-sided man Arizona has produced."
–William McLeod Raine

Indeed, Bucky was anything but one dimensional. He bent his curious mind to numerous studies including geology and history, and his his inherent drive to the purposes of one interest and project after another... often in an attempt to help people more than an attempt to make money. He spent much his time following his stint as sheriff, exploring and prospecting in the luminous bowels of the Grand Canyon, and as a result became passionate about its promotion as a tourist attraction as well as its protection for future generations.

From the time of the outlaws capture in '89 until his death, O'Neill has been held up by the promoters of a growing Arizona as an example of entrepreneurship, a business minded journalist, miner, investor, sheriff, judge and soldier. It is thus that he is portrayed in a life sized 1907 statue mounted on a pedestal in front of the Yavapai courthouse, on official county patches and a plaque in Washington's Arlington Cemetery, and on various tourist brochures drawing visitors to this day. But the fact is that he was elected to multiple public offices in spite of the efforts of the region's power brokers and major corporations to stop him. While he invested money in many industries including an ambitious water canal project, his vision for the region involved an economy based not on the polluting industries he'd witnessed in the East but non-typically on farming, crafts, retirement spas, and natural health resorts that he reasoned could bring in income without debasing area cultures and lifestyles.

Yes, he was a courageous fighter and flamboyant gambler, but he was also exceedingly bashful around strangers, terrified of public speaking, and tender in heart. While rock steady in a shootout, he was reported to have embarrassingly fainted while witnessing a public hanging, explaining later that he couldn't bear to see a man killed "without giving him a chance to fight for his life." Then, during the disembarking of the Rough Riders in the bay at Daiquiri on June 22, 1898, two negro Buffalo

Soldiers were seen to fall overboard and sink. Of all the men in the boat, it was only Bucky who defied the racial presuppositions of the day to leap in, with clothes and sword still on, in an unsuccessful bid to save them.

As caring a man as he was, O'Neill was equally unquenchable and untiring, a force of nature ready and excited for any seemingly worthwhile challenge. In his private and public life, he invariably defended the interests of the common folk against the power hungry "*corporados*" and stood tall for the oppressed, unmindful of the odds stacked against him. In this way, he remained an incurable gambler, bucking the political system and many cultural norms of the day, betting his very life on what he believed to be right.

There's a tomb in Section 1 of Arlington National Cemetery inscribed with a quote attributed to O'Neill: "Who would not die for a new star on the flag." This is an intentional alteration of a line spoken by O'Neill, in reply to a friend's remonstrations over his willingness to sign up with Roosevelt as a private: "Who wouldn't gamble for a star?" Business interests and economic boosters profess that he was referring to his beloved Arizona Territory winning the right to enter the Union as a state, but those who heard his remark at the time felt sure he was referring to winning himself a General's rank. Given the aforementioned troop toast, it was most likely a promotion that O'Neill was bucking for.

Either way, it was just like Bucky to bet first and foremost on his self, whether facing down robbers or standing up to legitimized robber-barons, attempting difficult daily tasks or trying to pull off the seemingly impossible. And such attitudes as his have emboldened at

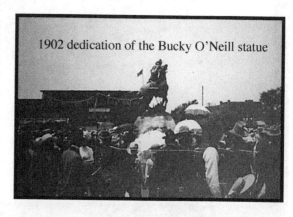

1902 dedication of the Bucky O'Neill statue

least a portion of every subsequent generation, helping in turn to form and further what I know to be the most definitive and admirable qualities of the iconic western character.

Chapter V

John Joshua Webb
& The Dodge City Gang

Robber With a Badge

J. J. Webb was an Old West officer of the law known for "working both sides" of it. Already well versed at both, once in Dodge City, Kansas he sold his services as a hired gun and rode with rustlers, yet also rode with Bat Masterson to bring other miscreants to ground. Moving on to the Southwest, he used his Marshall's office to shield the criminal acts of his larcenous associates.

My home state of New Mexico has distinguished itself with a history of official corruption far less subtle than the national average, being at times and in certain venues blunt and obvious enough to almost qualify as honest. From the machinations of the "Santa Fe Ring" that manipulated both politics and commerce in the 1870s and 80s to the more recent senatorial scandals of the state "Roundhouse," various cabals have used positions of power and prominence to ensure the security and profits of its privileged members with little visible attempt to conceal their methods or motives. Land belonging to the poor and uneducated has been repeatedly seized by large ranchers and developers who could count on the support of the local courts, monopolies have been enforced by driving out competition, and otherwise well meaning laws have been enforced unevenly in order to protect the elite and rid the territory of any who might challenge their rule or method. That said, never has there been an association of office holders and thieves more forthright than the "Dodge City Gang" during the period in which they ran roughshod over the population of Las Vegas, N.M. and its surrounding countryside.

> *"The [men of Las Vegas] are as tough a bunch of bad men as ever gathered outside a penal institution!"*
> –Miguel Otero, Territorial Governor

Situated in the Northeast quadrant of the state, this Las Vegas existed 70 years before the mobster Dutch Schultz launched Nevada's now world famous capital of gambling, and for a time was the most populated city between California and Missouri. It lay nestled between two ecosystems – the pine covered Sangre de Christo mountains and the Great Plains, Christened *Nuestra Senora de los Dolores de Las Vegas Grandes* (Lady of Sorrows of the Grand Meadows) in the 1600s, in 1834 it became the last Spanish colony in North America when so chartered by Spain. It served both as a trading center and fort in cases of Apache attack, quickly growing to several thousand residents including adventurers, entrepreneurs and desperadoes all looking for new venues and experiences, business opportunities or "easy pickins". Water issues as well as land issues marked this as a land of conflict from the start, exacerbated by the mixed-blessing arrival of the Atchison, Topeka, & Santa Fe railroad on July 4th, 1879.

The trains brought with them not only chances for increased prosperity and exchange, but also camps full of railway workers and the prostitutes to tend their needs, carloads of land sharks and outlaws on the lam. At one time or another Billy the Kid, Hook-Nosed Jim, Doc Holliday and Big-Nosed Kate, Cock-Eyed Frank, Vincente Silva and the White Caps Gang, Monte Verde, The Durango Kid, Bob Ford and even Jesse James himself either visited or resided in Las Vegas, referred to in the New York newspapers "the baddest of the bad" towns. The tracks were laid through the eastern end of town, bypassing the old downtown and its plaza in the west end, the western section being comprised mainly of

John "Doc" Holliday

peaceful residents and the east with its railway development became the headquarters for thuggery. Conflicts between the two communities and crimes in the east half had turned so bloody in the months following the railway's arrival, that citizen Vigilance Committees were formed.

Officially commissioned to uphold the law and protect its citizens in East Las Vegas was the marshal, Joe Carson, soon followed by John Joshua Webb. What they actually upheld was the right of the associates and allies a man who was conveniently not only the mayor of East Las Vegas but its Justice of the Peace and Coroner, Hyman Neill – alias "Hoodoo Brown" – to prey on the community with impunity.

John was born in the not-so-West state of Iowa, in Keokuk County on the 14th of February, 1847. His parents took him to Nebraska in 1862 and he left the Midwest for good in 1871, working as a surveyor, buffalo hunter, teamster and then police officer in eastern Colorado, Wyoming, South Dakota, Kansas and New Mexico. While of average height, his strong build, chiseled facial features and forceful nature marked him as someone to be reckoned with. Early on he grew a trademark long beard and mustache, while keeping the sides of his face cleanly shaved, and preferred to a dapper jacket and waist-coat to the work clothes more common to the area. As with other notables such as Tom Horn, Pat Garrett and Buckshot Roberts, it was his willingness and ability to wield a gun that earned him the most respect and largest checks. Besides performing secretive "hits" for various private employers, he was also often picked by the authorities to ride with their posses when on especially dangerous missions. In 1877 he was deputized by Ford County Sheriff Charlie Bassett and sent with under-Sheriff Bat Masterson on futile search for the train robber Sam Bass.

Soon after Bat was elected to replace Sheriff Bassett in 1878, Webb was again deputized to assist with hunting down another batch of train robbers, including Edgar West and "Dirty Dave" Rudabaugh. Four days later the posse cornered the gang, and Webb supposedly got the drop on Rudabaugh just he reached for his revolver. Dave was said to have proved how "Dirty" he was by turning informant the same day he got locked into his cell, spilling the beans on their remaining accomplices in exchange for his release, and promising to go straight. Straight he went, though only straight to New Mexico and yet another series of crimes, and this time in league with Webb instead of hunted by him. Does that make you wonder whether both the arrest and release might have been for some reason staged?

In the Fall of 1878, John was commissioned by the commander of Fort Dodge, Lieutenant Colonel William Henry Lewis, to join the famous manhunter Bill Tilgham and other frontiersmen on a scout for hostile Indians who had escaped the reservation. Chief Dull Knife's intentions were only to get back to their homelands, not to raid white settlements,, and the impromptu scouts including Webb were soon mustered out.

In early 1879 he was one of many notorious gunmen hired by the Atchison, Topeka & Santa Fe to enforce a right-of-way through Colorado's Royal Gorge claimed by the rival Denver & Rio Grande Railway, going so far as to seize and fortify Denver & Rio Grande stations along the line. Each side fielded a few dozen well armed denizens of the West to shoot the piss out of each other should the negotiations fail, but amazingly there was only one fatality before a negotiated settlement was arranged. In spite of having failed to earn their bonuses, Webb somehow found the money to purchase a Las Vegas saloon on Center Street only a few months later... in partnership with the equally shady but far more elegant dentist, gambler and gunman John Henry "Doc" Holliday.

What wasn't known was that Webb and Holliday had the backing of Webb's Dodge City cohort, Hoodoo Brown, along with some of the most powerful figures in the county. John was by that time a full fledged member of the Dodge City Gang, the coalition of well-heeled scoundrels that included not only rustlers, robbers and gunmen, but also well-placed judges and lawyers, money-laundering bankers, regional real estate moguls, and the Marshal... all with connections to Dodge City. Its leader, Hoodoo Brown made management decisions as the east-side's Mayor, jailed his enemies and exonerated his cohorts as Justice of the Peace, and as Coroner was the one who determined whether or not a gunshot victim had been killed in "self defense." His appointed City Marshal was Joe Carson, his right hand man, assisted by Deputy U. S. Marshal "Mysterious Dave" Mather, special policeman J. J. Webb and a host of professional gunmen and thieves including Selim K. "Frank" Cady, William P. "Slap Jack Bill" Nicholson, "Dutchy" Schunderberger, John "Bull Shit Jack" Pierce and "Dirty Dave" Rudabaugh. Yes, this is the same Dirty Dave that Webb was said to have earlier arrested, with both of them now working for the same ambitious boss. Smell something fishy? Boss Hyman "Hoodoo Brown" Neill hailed from Missouri, but ran away to Kansas as a young man to haul lumber and hunt buffalo like Webb, and creatively tried his hand at managing a traveling opera company in old Mexico.

Some said that Neill got his name "Hoodoo Brown" from one of his girls-of-the-line, and that it referred to the "bad luck" that he brought with him, while others asserted that it referred to his dabbling in the occult "dark arts" to ensure the success of his foul deeds. Whatever else he was up to, Brown is known to have led the Gang in the commission of well planned burglaries, extortion, train and stagecoach robberies, and even murders throughout the years 1879 and '80.

Hoodoo Brown as Video Game character

Meanwhile on July 19th of '79 Mike Gordon, a well liked but love-drunk resident of West Las Vegas, made the mistake of trying to coax one of Webb and Holliday's "ladies of the night" into leaving with him, claiming that the intimacy of the paid-for pokes were somehow evidence of her hidden affections. Webb ordered the drunken Gordon to leave the saloon, whereupon the darkly gallant 100 pound Holliday followed him out and administered a drawl-filled tongue lashing. Doc taunted the sodbuster Gordon until he pulled his revolver and let off a wild shot, after which the homicidal tooth-puller pulled his own handgun and sent three far more accurate rounds into the frustrated suitor's belly. Threats of a hanging by West Las Vegas vigilantes reached the saloon keepers within hours of the deed, prompting Holliday to transfer his share of the business to Webb, and then follow his friend the bunko artist Wyatt Earp to Tombstone and what would only two years later be the "shootout at the O.K. Corral."

Webb managed the saloon by himself until early 1880, at which time Marshall Joe Carson was shot and killed in an altercation in the Close & Patterson Variety Hall. On January 22nd, cowboys John Dorsey, James West, William Randall and T.J. House had been out having a good time "shooting the moon" when they decided to enter the hall and join the dance that was in progress there. The Gang member and marshall somewhat hypocritically demanded that they obey the new gun control ordinance and turn in their weapons, a demand that apparently went over like a lead balloon. In the melee that followed, Carson was killed with a shot to the head, as UnderSheriff "Mysterious" Dave Mather put holes in two of the opposing revelers. Mather was appointed as Marshall immediately thereafter, and John Webb was named city policeman.

"Mysterious Dave" Mather

House and the wounded Dorsey escaped out the door, but on the 5th of February Hoodoo learned they were laying low north of the city in Buena Vista, at the *casa* of one Juan Antonio Dominguez. He instructed Webb to lead a posse including Dirty Dave and five others. Surrounding the pair, Webb promised them safe passage and a fair trial. There were, however, broken out of the jail and hung from the town's infamous and ever busy windmill gallows, by masked men who may have belonged to the Vigilance Committee based in West Las Vegas, but who were more likely were in Hoodoo's employ. Carson's enraged widow was said to have taken pot shots at the doomed men, though whether before or after they were strung up was never made clear.

In the following eight weeks Officer Webb was suspected by the populous of participating in or covering up a number of new crimes, further stirring the vigilante passions. Then on March 9, 1880, an incident occurred that drove the Committee to take concerted action... the so called "straw that broke the camel's back." The rumor in town was that Hoodoo Brown had heard that local cattleman Michael Kelliher was making the rounds of the saloons with over a thousand dollars on his person – an enormous amount at that time – and that Hoodoo had ordered Marshall Carson, Webb and Mather to seize these funds by whatever means necessary. True or not, it was at least a case of selective enforcement when at around 4:00 that morning – according to an article in the Las Vegas Optic – Kelliher and friends were approached by the lawmen in the Gang-owned Goodlet & Roberts' Saloon and ordered to turn over their handguns. A gun control ordinance was recently put in effect, but very few citizens paid any attention to it, there was little previous enforcement, and several others in the bar were also openly carrying their Colts and Smith & Wessons.

The Optic newspaper received considerable advertising and other funding from Hoodoo Brown, which may or may not explain their uncritically reporting the officer's version. According to them, Kelliher belligerently shouted "I won't be disarmed - everything goes!" and then made a grab for his revolver. According to this report, Webb was simply too fast on the draw for him, though there was no explanation in the paper of how Kelliher could have been shot twice in the chest and a then a final round to the head without ever having gotten his gun out of its holster. The people of Las Vegas were less convinced than the Optic's correspondent, however, especially after hearing the victim's money had

somehow managed to disappear between the time the body was picked up off the Goodlet & Roberts oaken floor and when it was deposited on an examination table in Hoodoo's office of the Coroner. An angry mob quickly formed outside the jail, demanding that Webb be turned over to them for summary justice, but they were held at bay by Hoodoo's rifle toting men, hard cases headed by Webb's supposed enemy, Dirty Dave Rudabaugh.

"Dirty Dave" Rudabaugh

In response, on the 8th of April, 1880 this group of fed-up citizens paid for the following attention-getting notice in the Las Vegas Optic newspaper, addressing all manner of criminals but directed primarily at the hated Dodge City Gang:

TO MURDERERS, CONFIDENCE MEN, THIEVES: "*The citizens of Las Vegas have tired of robbery, murder, and other crimes that have made this town a byword in every civilized community. They have resolved to put a stop to crime, if in attaining that end they have to forget the law and resort to a speedier justice than it will afford. All such characters are therefore, hereby notified, that they must either leave this town or conform themselves to the requirements of law, or they will be summarily dealt with. The flow of blood must and shall be stopped in this community, and the good citizens of both the old and new towns have determined to stop it, if they have to hang by the strong arm of force every violator of the law in this country.*"

-Vigilantes

While no historian I know of has ever guessed as much, it seems likely that Webb may have been used as a traditional "fall guy," a scapegoat meant to draw both the public's and the Vigilante Committee's attention away from Hoodoo Brown Neill whom so many in the area considered ultimately responsible. If so, the agreement with Webb may have included a promise to spring him from the hoosegow, since in April of 1880 Hoodoo's men Dirty Dave Rudabaugh and Little Jack Allen attempted to break him out. Dave found it easy to shoot down the much loved jailer Deputy Antonio Lino Valdez, but still found himself unable to open the locks to free Webb.

The "Hanging Windmill" – Las Vegas, N.M.
–Vigilante Venue–

Knowing that the Vigilance Committee was sure to react, Hoodoo likely cautioned Rudabaugh and Allen to hide out for awhile, and they and Tom Pickett rode off to the southwest that very night. There first stop was the Thomas Yerby ranch in the Fort Sumner area where they posed as working cowboys. Sometime later, Dirty Dave shot and killed Allen, whom he had reason to fear was planning to betray him. Then in late May, he and Pickett were introduced to Billy the Kid by Billy confidante Charlie Bowdre. They participated in a number of cattle rustling raids before, on the 27th of November, Dave, Billy Wilson and the Kid killed Deputy James Carlyle. Then on the 19th of December, 1880, Sheriff-elect Pat Garrett and his posse ambushed Billy and his party, ventilating compatriot Tom O'Folliard. Four days later they engaged them again, killing Charlie Bowdre and capturing Billy, Pickett, Wilson and Rudabaugh. Meanwhile back in Las Vegas, the Vigilantes were having a grand ol' time rounding up or chasing off every violator of the peace that they could get hold of, all the time isolating and putting the pressure on head honcho Hoodoo Brown Neill. In December, Brown is indicted for the theft of Kelliher's money and quickly goes into hiding.

In February of 1881, Dave is given a 99 year prison sentence for theft of the U.S. Mails during a train robbery, followed soon after by a death sentence for the murder of Deputy Valdez.

Sheriff John Webb with leg irons, Las Vegas N.M. Jail

Then on the 19th of September, Webb joined his fellow prisoners Dave Rudabaugh, A. Murphy, H. S. Wilson and Thomas Duffy, either picking the lock of their cell or more likely being smuggled a key as well as a pistol by Hoodoo allies. A scuffle with the three guards ensues in which Duffy is killed and Webb, Rudabaugh, Wilson, and Murphy are beaten and tossed back into their confines.

Less than two months later, on the 2nd of December, Webb, Rudabaugh and five others finished scraping out the mortar around a 7" x 19" building block in the wall and flee the area. It seems beyond belief that given the reputations of the inmates and their recent escape attempts, the jailers would fail to have them on constant watch, or that they were unable to hear the scraping of tools against concrete for the many days it would have taken to complete the task and remove the stone. More likely their guards had been paid to ignore the sounds, either by Hoodoo Brown who was in hiding, or some of their supporters.

Within a week following the escape Hoodoo was seen in Houston, and was soon after arrested for the murder of a Las Vegas deputy who had been killed under mysterious circumstances a few months before. It looked especially suspicious to Houston observers when the deputy's widow traveled to Texas to visit Brown in his cell, and fell immediately into his amorous arms... or as the Parsons Sun newspaper put it: "The meeting between the pair is said to have been affecting in the extreme, and rather more affectionate than would be expected under the circumstances." It appeared the charges include adultery and theft as well as murder until two local attorneys he hired made the point that the Texas courts had no authority to hold him and no interstate extradition agreements were yet in effect. Brown was released, whereupon according to the Chicago Times he and the widow were witnessed "skylarking through some of the interior towns of Kansas" before settling in Mexico with this or another common-law wife. According to Hyman "Hoodoo Brown" Neill's descendants, he died in Torreon, Cuahuila. Historical researchers uncovered the existence of an Elizabeth Brown who had moved a while after to Leadville, Colorado, who had a reputation for dabbling in the "dark arts" and may or may not have been the wife and partner of Hoodoo.

After the escape in '81, Dirty Dave made his way West to Tombstone, Arizona where he sided with the Clanton gang against the Earp brothers, and where he very probably participated in the ambushes of both Virgil and Morgan. Some writers have suggested that he spent some time below the border before running a herd of stolen cattle to Montana, raising three daughters and finally dying in 1928 a lonely alcoholic Oregon rancher. According to most reports, however, in February of 1886 Rudabaugh was playing poker in a cantina in Parral, Mexico when the villagers he was cheating stood up to protest.

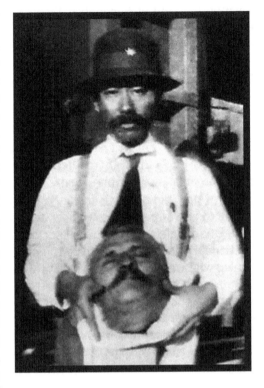

Dave was said to have shot one hombre through the head and sent a second bullet crashing through the heart of a second man. According to this version a whiskeyed-up Rudabaugh was unable to find where he'd tied his horse in the moonless night and then made the mistake of returning to the adobe saloon, now appearing ominous with all its kerosene lamps blown out. The villagers may have then swarmed and killed the *muy mal* Americano outlaw. Certainly for years after, tourists visiting the area could purchase postcard photos reputed to be of Dirty Dave's severed noggin, paraded around on a pole mustachio and all, then displayed like a pig's head at a festival feast.

The fugitive lawman John Joshua Webb may have fared better, first escaping to Kansas under the pseudonym "Samuel King," then on to Winslow, Arkansas as a railroad guard. He probably caught a severe case of smallpox in 1882, finally receiving a death sentence that none but Providence could commute.

In this 21st Century it is rare but not unheard of for cliques of lawmen to band together to rob drug dealers of their money, and for judges to cover for them either out of blind faith in their officers, or the fear of undermining the legal system with the exposure of police malpractice. Much more common is a kind of selective law enforcement that imposes heavily on the underclass, minorities and the poor but is seldom applied to the wealthy and influential. Land sharks continue to prey on the vulnerable and uninformed, undoing historic land grants, taxing poor neighborhoods until the buildings can be repossessed and renovated. The law of "imminent domain" is used not only to take possession of private properties needed for public roads, but to seize it for sale to private industries that a city finds desirable. I believe the "black arts" that Hoodoo Brown was accused of can now serve as a euphemism for politics: the art of deception, manipulation and appropriation. We have reason to fear the extremes of unthinking vigilantism, but no more so than theft and oppression made systematic and institutional. For all the Las Vegas Vigilance Committee's excesses, it proved an able check on official corruption, and the town was soon able to resume its role as a bucolic, culture filled setting for honest labors and the raising of families.

It is up to each of us as sovereign and conscientious beings to choose what role models we aspire to, whether it be the dishonest, system-ensconced John Webbs of the world or the honorable Bat Mastersons, freedom loving edge-dwellers and staunch individualists. National governments, states, provinces and their law enforcement agencies have a mandate to serve and protect their populations, but as always it is the individual – the individual citizen as well as sheriff or policeman – who has the responsibility to personally measure the fairness and applicability of its laws, applaud its most just intentions and acts, and resist its inevitable injustices.

Chapter VI

Wild Bill Hickok

The Real Deal

"August 1st, 1876..." he wrote at the top of the letter, and then an ornately lettered "Dear Agnes" before dipping his pen back into the open bottle of india ink. Agnes was his wife, a large and by no means typically attractive divorcee some years his senior, but throughout their five years of courting and only five months of marriage he had thought of her as his one and only beloved. Upon closer inspection, it suddenly seems obvious what attracted the gunman to her and finally moved him to settle down – for her daring and verve were every bit the match of his, as an accomplished circus performer, trick bareback rider and fearless lion tamer. She had no similar penchant to tame her Wild Bill, yet no doubt worried that his leaving her to make money to build them a home wasn't also an excuse for him to delay the domestic life and take refuge in the danger filled sporting world again. We can only imagine what she might have felt, upon discovering that her husband's words were not only dramatic expression of his devotion, but premonition and portent.

"Darling, if such should be we should never meet again, while firing my last shot I will gently breathe the name of my wife – Agnes – and with wishes even for my enemies, I will make the plunge and try to swim to the other shore."

The signature was formal, as typical of the times. J.B. Hickok, it said, and only a day after mailing that letter, Wild Bill lay dead... with his boots on like he'd predicted, and a ragged hole through his head.

James Butler, one of the truly most formidable gunslingers of the Old West, proved right about a few other things as well. It was not face to face against aggressive opponents where lay danger and his destiny, but in betrayal and ambush, in the kind of scurrilous attack coming not from in front but from behind. Hickok, the archetypal stand-up fighter, was killed while seated... at a   poker table, while admonishing a Missouri River steamboat captain to stop peeking at the pile of discards. And he died with his back unusually exposed, after having been jokingly refused his customary seat with its back safely to the wall.

Hickok's body arched backwards, tipping the chair and hitting the hardwood floor, along with the cards that he'd been holding: a pair of aces and a pair of eights along with one other, to be known for generations to come as the "Dead Man's Hand." Still holstered on his wide frontiersman's belt were what his friend at the time described as Colt conversions, front loading Army or Navy model percussion revolvers that had been altered to accept .38 caliber, breech loaded

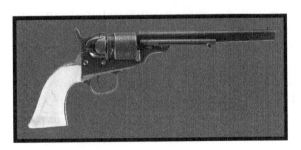

metallic cartridges. If so, they would have been chosen so as to retain the familiar feel and excellent balance of the percussion Colts he had carried and treasured throughout his life.

While the .45 Colt Peacemaker of 1872 had been introduced four years earlier, it hadn't yet begun to compete with the practical and inexpensive surplus arms released following the war between the states. In addition, the older technology utilized loose balls and powder, making it possible to easily cast one's bullets, whereas the newfangled factory-made metallic cartridges were much more expensive to shoot and harder to find. So attached was Bill to his Colt Navies, in fact, that he likely sold and certainly seldom if ever carried the innovative Smith & Wesson #3 top break revolvers presented to him by fellow thespian William "Buffalo Bill" Cody.

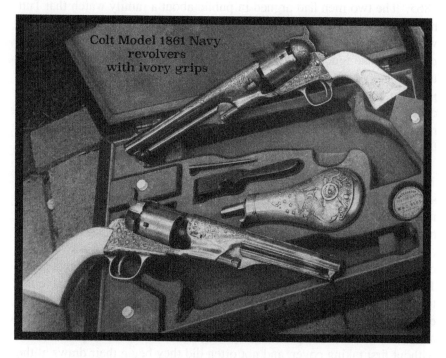

Colt Model 1861 Navy revolvers with ivory grips

The 1851 Colt "Navy" Model that was Hickok's favorite, was so named because of the naval battle scene roll engraved on its cylinders. The "Navy" was favored by many over the other Colt six-shooters of the series, the behemoth .44 Dragoon and .44 caliber 1860 Model New Army, as being possibly more durable than the latter and verifiably lighter and more balanced. As with all such revolvers, black powder was first poured into the cylinders, then a lead ball dropped on top of each and firmly rammed home by a pivoting lever beneath the barrel. A dob of grease was usually packed over the bullet in each cylinder to guard against flying sparks, followed last by the placement of percussion primer caps over the nipples at the rear. It is said that Hickok practiced often with his, so that he could hit nearly equally well with either hand. And because of black powder's tendency to absorb moisture and misfire, he was heard to empty this handguns every evening by shooting into an alley, starting each day with confidence with his freshened loads.

Contrary to some versions of the story, it was evidently a Colt Navy that ended his hopes for a life with Agnes, and it was most certainly a Navy as well that Hickok employed to kill his friend and fellow gambler, Dave Tutt, with a remarkable 75 yard heart shot on the evening of July 21st, 1865. The two men had argued in public about a family watch that Tutt had taken from Bill as collateral against a gambling debt, Bill had warned him not to wear it in public until they settled, and an equally proud Tutt had ignored him. It was just after 6 pm when the two of them unexpectedly encountered each other, entering from opposite sides of the plaza in front of the Springfield, Missouri courthouse. "Dave, don't cross that square with my watch!", Hickok shouted, setting both men to reach for their guns in what was to serve as the model for the archetypal fair fight, face to face quickdraw shootouts on hurriedly emptying streets.

The Hickok/Tutt fight was, in fact, one the only documented incidents of such a confrontation in the entire annals of the American West, with the majority of altercations involving one or the other party initiating the trouble with a surprise attack or carefully planned ambuscade. Most often the participants were drunk, unexpectedly banging away at each other over some perceived slight at distances of only one to six feet apart. That there weren't more deaths in those wooly days, was attributable not to either civilized restraint or gun control ordinances and law enforcement, but by the poor aim of the inebriated. Other than the Tuck and Hickok case, hardly ever did protagonists meet in the open and fire without first taking cover, and not often did they begin their draws at the same time. Here was a truly remarkable confrontation between equally brave men, unbowed veterans of the recent national conflagration, one good and one evil it was said, nursing grudges and ready at the drop of a hat to defend their honor and reputations with lead... the story upon which the most oft repeated of Western legends is based. This is the gunfight retold in a million ways to suit the teller and sell their magazines and papers, recast as the white hats and black hats of early simplistic Western movies and television series, sanitized and simplified for the kid's comics of the 1940s through 60s, and then dirtied up but nonetheless misrepresented by the hard cussing TV of the 21st Century.

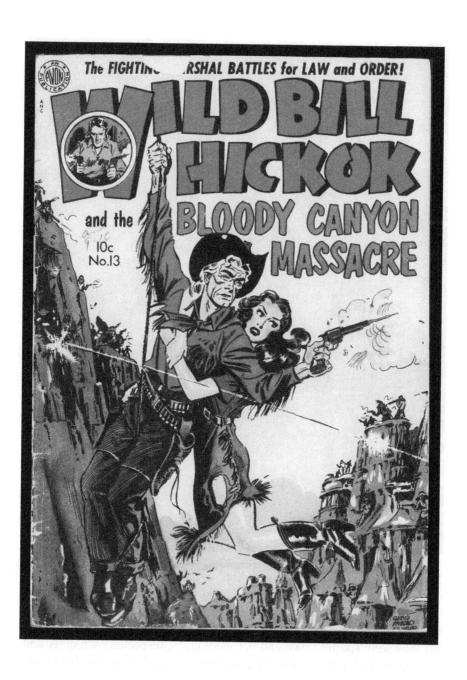

Needless to say, most of the accounts were embellished or inflated and real fights seldom happened as portrayed. But more tellingly, not even the Tutt/Hickok fight itself went down quite the way we might think. Hickok had served the army of the North and Tutt with the Confederacy, but they were sporting men and not ideologues, respected each other and were genuine friends, with the only reason one had to die being the pridefulness of the two men and the values and customs of their age. And it was anything but a quick draw match, with both men needing time to extricate their Colts – Hickock's perhaps from a trademark sash, Tutt's likely from a protective full-flap holster held high and tight to the waist rather than slung low and tied down like those onscreen. Both men fired at almost the same time, deliberate, aimed fire from eye level and not snap shots from the hip. Tutt had even turned sideways, in true 18th Century duelist fashion. His shot missed, while Hickok's found its mark.

If anything, Hickok warned against fast drawing and firing, advising anyone "getting in a row" to "take time... I've known many a feller to slip up for shootin' in a hurry." And while he dropped Tutt at the 75 yard mark, the other nine or so that he sent to their cowboy Valhalla were whacked at close range. Stories that he could hit an object thrown in the air with every shot from his two revolvers, were balanced by more sober reports that he could quickly place all 12 shots inside a foot-wide board at 50 yards... more than adequate, nonetheless, in any real-world gunfight. And what he had equal to or in excess of all other contemporary gunmen, was that quality I have spoken of elsewhere: deliberation... being able to make calm clear decisions and act unhesitatingly in the face of mortal threat. This he had in spades, along with an instinctual willingness to do whatever it takes whenever he thought himself right, even the taking of a life.

Bill's service in the Union had included not only scouting, but also assignment as a detective for the Union's Provost Marshall, convincing him he might be suited to make his living as a civilian by putting on a badge. Here seemed a way for a self described "man of action" to be in the thick of the excitement, while remaining on the "right" side of the law. His broad shoulders, unflappable demeanor, unquestionable courage and great skill with firearms did indeed well qualify him for the dangerous job, which mostly entailing riding herd on rowdy party goers and

visiting miscreants and sociopaths. With his combined wild courage and reputation for honesty he's truly one of the most laudable as well as formidable examples of Western lawman that we have, even though he only had a star pinned on for a relatively short amount of time total: intermittent work as a Deputy U.S. Marshall in Kansas between 1865 and 1871, one year as the elected acting sheriff of Ellis County, Kansas, and filling in for eight months as the Chief of Police of Abilene Texas in 1870 after Marshall "Bear River" Smith was killed there. And as honest, imposing and effective as he could be, he still wasn't very good at either getting elected or hanging on to appointments. He lost his Ellis County position in the first general election, and was fired in Abilene for having jailed or bludgeoned so many Texas drovers that the city was losing their business.

It was, in fact, immediately after the sting of losing his first ever stab at winning a job in law enforcement – the position of City Marshall of Springfield – that he gave the interview which would introduce his exaggerated persona to the world. Bill always was a yarn spinner, as folks were called who told outrageous stories as a practiced form of campfire or fireplace entertainment, but this time he may also have been trying to make himself feel better after his political defeat. Or it could have been solely the prevarications of the interviewer and author, Col. George Nichols, correspondent for the exceedingly popular Harper's New Monthly Magazine, as he sculpted the truth in the interest of the most dramatic possible effect on his urbane readers. Bill's family recalled that he was none too pleased about the more patently ridiculous stories that Nichols included in his series, but America and even Europe ate it up. Over the remaining 10 years of his life, Hickok both exploited the ensuing reputation – such as when attempting to awe would-be lawbreakers into behaving – and also suffered for it, by forever after literally needing to guard his back against those who were envious and resentful of that reputation.

The earliest and most controversial shooting situation that Bill ever got into occurred on July 12, 1861, when he backed up the current proprietors of the isolated Rock Creek relay station, Horace Wellman and family, against an irate David McCanless arriving to repossess it. In Col. Nichols' version for Harpers in 1867, no mention is made of the dispute over legal ownership which triggered it all. And the way he describes it, Bill jumped to the aid of an innocent family against a large band of murdering cutthroats, managing with but a single revolver and bowie knife to shoot or slash to death all ten! In reality, only the hearty 6' tall McCanless and his 12 year old boy had approached the station's door, with Dave having left his two employees to stay in the barn with the horses. He was shot in the chest in the middle of loudly arguing his point with the grown Wellman daughter Jane, fired either by Hickok or the old man Wellman who had been concealed behind a curtain. Either way, it was likely Bill's least laudable scrape, as they then shot McCanless' two hired hands running to investigate, watching as the maddened Jane finished one off with a hoe and then tried in vain to catch and club the fast retreating little boy.

More wholly defendable, was Hickok's next celebrated fight, in "Paddy Welch's" saloon in Hay's City. The press of the time, including the Kansas City Daily Commonwealth, reported that he had repelled an attack by five members of the 7th Cavalry, and the book by Buell, "Heroes of The Plains", put the number at 15. But as much as the facts can be known, it would seem the actual encounter involved only two. The first of these, a powerfully built soldier by the name of Lonergan, was both a onetime Medal of Honor winner and a recent army deserter, and had taken offense at something Bill had said. For the first but not last time, Hickok was taken from behind, with Lonergan prudently pinning his arms to the side and falling with him to the floor.

His fellow deserter, Kelly, then stepped over with his cocked Remington revolver, placed it against Bill's temple and pulled the trigger. The hammer fell with a loud click instead of a bang, the shot having misfired to Hickok's great relief. Bill had managed to snake his own gun out of its holster by that point, and was just able to cock his wrist enough to get off a shot into Kelly's gun hand and then another into his side. With Kelly out of the action, Bill struggled to get the barrel pointed behind him at Lonergan, finally blasting away his knee cap and thereby breaking free. He then leapt through the nearest window without bothering to open it, taking the curtain with him as he made his strategic withdrawal. My fellow firearms historian, Joseph Rosa, has pointed out how fortunate Hickok was that Kelly had used a government issued Remington New Army .44 with a reputation for occasional malfunctions, instead of possibly more reliable Colt.

It is known that Hickok owned not only his Colt Navies, but also a Sharps breech loading carbine that was for awhile buried with him, and usually an interesting pair of derringers that he apparently never had the occasion to fire in anger. The Williamsons looked a lot like the earlier trademark muzzle loading derringers, with the bonus that they were clever breech loaders that could either fire either a .41 caliber metallic cartridge, or with the aid of a special brass insert, fire loose powder and ball. It was, however, his silver plated, ivory stocked Colt Navies that he put to work in what turned out to be his final gunfight.

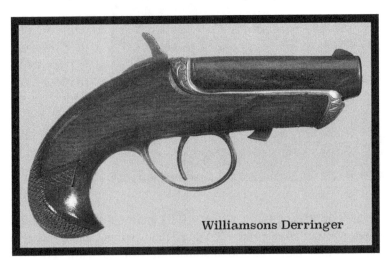

Williamsons Derringer

The encounter took place on October 5th, 1871, in Abilene, Texas, where Bill had been appointed acting Chief of Police. While that other noted lawman Wyatt Earp was known to operate brothels between shootouts,

Hickok got in trouble for enforcing regulations against prostitution and shutting the red light district down. But just like Earp, the shootout with the greatest unintended ramifications was triggered (pardon the pun) by his enforcement of unpopular new gun control ordinances. Combined with the fact that he was a northerner in a position of authority a southern town, his roughshod arrests of partying cowboys – simply for packing iron – had in only eight months of service resulted in numerous death threats... including one by Texan Phil Coe, who let it be known he'd put an end to Hickok by "first frost".

It was around 8 at night that Hickok was heard warning a growing crowd of disgruntled Texans not to be caught carrying firearms within the city limits. He'd only been gone an hour when he heard a pistol shot ring out from the same spot. Running with his Colts in hand, he found Coe at the head of those gathered, his revolver still smoking. "I was just shooting at a stray dog," he supposedly explained, before bringing his guns up to waist level and firing. Hickock immediately returned the shots thrusting both arms straight out and putting twin .36 caliber balls into Coe's gut. Just as quickly, he blasted a second armed man running towards him in the dark, only this time it wasn't another riotous Texas drover but Mike Williams, his deputy and friend. He must have known he did the natural thing, that if he didn't react without hesitation he might have been overtaken by an adversary and died. That said, it would be the last man ever shot by James Butler Hickok, and for two days the usually stoic gunman cried.

Hopefully he made it to whatever "shore" he had in mind, when five years later he wrote his dear Agnes those prophetic last lines. Either way, we can be sure that he died ready for the "plunge." He always was. Hickok may have been one of the least corrupted of Old West lawdogs, sometimes enforcing the kinds of regulations that both I and those feisty Texans find deplorable, but at the same time refusing the usual bribes, facing danger head on, going to the aid of the weak and the victimized and standing resolutely at their side. And Wild Bill may come the closest of all the old time gunfighters, when it comes to genuinely living up to an impossibly large and in his case un-survivable reputation... a complex man, truly worthy of a legend.

Chapter VII

Pat Garrett

Possibly Less Admirable Than The Killers He Chased

If there is any one thing imparted by these varied stories of famous lawmen, it is that both the most laudable and least respectable among them were naught but fellow human beings, affected by insecurities and fears, balancing personal needs with the requirements of others, making choices that are sometimes honorable and at other times expedient or even despicable. Like us, they were an amalgam of easily recognizable qualities as well as generally less commendable traits, with moments of apparent selfishness as well as times of unqualified magnanimity, responding to sometimes difficult situations that they may or may not have helped create. They walked the forked path of life not as gods but as thoroughly mortal men, not yet fossilized and enshrined as sacred myths that generations of people would fear to question or challenge. Unlike the mythic and supernatural, they were gunslingers who didn't always hit the target, sometimes shot the wrong person by accident or on purpose, and on occasion – at least in the case of Wyatt Earp's brother Morgan – entered into a gunfight without remembering to first load their gun. They pulled their pants on one leg at a time the same way we do, and sometimes made regretful sounds in public. And just like us, they would inevitably need to stop every few hours when on long trips in order to relieve themselves... or as folks were more likely to say back then, to "catch some scenery," "water the cactus" or "bleed the lizard".

Proud onetime Sheriff, Pat Garrett, was doing just exactly that on the side of the Mail-Scott Road, when on March 1st, 1908 near New Mexico's Alameda Arroyo, the over six feet tall lawman – known to most only as "the man who killed Billy The Kid" – took a bullet through the back of his head.

The ex-lawman had proved demonstrably human in other ways as well, being at 57 years old an alcoholic deeply in debt, cohabiting with a prostitute while his own family did without, called troublesome and "one mean S.O.B" by even his most loyal of sympathizers and supporters. His reputation as the Kid's lawful executioner had done nothing to enrich him and won him criticism from much of the Southwest's population, and now years later he was considered still dangerous if near friendless.

It was not, however, the beginning of Pat Garrett's disrepute. His indisputable courage and doggedness as a manhunter can only be fairly measured against a lifetime of questionable values and unsavory acts, from his betrayal of his friend The Kid to his mercenary tendencies, ornery temper and outright dishonesty, a gambling addiction as well as an embittered craving for the kinds of riches, power and privilege he could never claim. Pat envied the upper crust of agrarian based society with their easily won incomes and ability to curry political favors, any yet he proved ill suited for both business and public office. He continued to serve the elite's vested interests, however, right up until such time as they had completely distanced themselves from him over his drunkenness, thievery, or consistent failure to pay back his personal debts. Entitled, arrogant and unusually tall, he was the kind of fellow that littler men like Billy might well love to kick.

Patrick Floyd Garrett's troublesome life began in Chambers County, Alabama on June 5th of 1850. When he was six, his parents moved with him on to a Claiborne Parish plantation in northern Louisiana. Their fortunes declined under the conditions of the post Civil War reconstruction era. Then, in 1869, the explosive 19 year old threatened to kill a brother-in-law for doing commerce with the hated northern "carpetbaggers," those opportunistic investors rushing to the southern states to take advantage of the dissolute there and amass their properties. Whether to spare his sister the grief or to avoid what could be a deadly fight, Garrett left home immediately afterwards, first working as a cowpuncher in Texas' Dallas area, and then hunting some of the last remaining buffalo herds for their hides up in the Texas panhandle. He shot and killed his first man in 1878, a fellow hunter he was arguing with over the ownership of some of these hides, and a fellow who should have known better than to bring a camp axe to a gunfight. He next pushed on west into New Mexico, where he briefly worked for Pete Maxwell before being fired for rustling cattle, the same Maxwell Ranch where he would later ambush William "Billy" Bonney/Antrim, otherwise known as the Kid. That same year, he is said to have partnered with the Kid and another rustler by the name of Barney Mason, gathering a sufficient number of other people's cows to open up his own saloon, quickly becoming a drinking hangout for the majority of the local outlaws. Being such a "tall drink of water," he soon got the nickname of Juan Largo (Long John), and he and Billy were sometimes called "Big Casino" and "Little Casino" because of their size difference when standing together at the bar. Two years later he married Apolonaria Guiterrez, and they industriously went to work making the first of what would be a total of nine Garrett children.

The sheriff of Lincoln County, New Mexico, George Kimbell, resigned on November 7th, 1880, two months before his term officially ended. As Kimbell's successor, The Democrat-run county temporarily appointed Garrett to fill in, and then pushed him to run for the job as a Democrat even though Pat had always been a Republican... not because of his upstanding morals, but precisely because he knew and had the trust of the area's miscreants, in particular Billy The Kid, who was by that point wanted for murder for his part in what would later be known as the Lincoln County War. He'd handed out booze and cigars at the area bars, and bragged about his quick gun, but everyone knew it was Billy who had inadvertently won him the election.

Lew Wallace, the governor of New Mexico territory at the time, sided with the corrupt "Santa Fe Gang" of lawyers and politicians that essentially controlled both commerce and elections in the future state, and against all those seeking justice and redress, including the Kid. The cash reward Wallace posted for Billy's killing or capture inspired the first posse to go on the search, but while they did overtake the Kid and friends, they only

managed to shoot to pieces one of their own men, Jim Carlisle, during failed negotiations.

Pat Garrett would prove more effective, largely because he already knew and had himself used most of the region's outlaw hideouts, during his own recent period of cattle thieving. And he knew just who to ask, to get the information he needed to track his old drinking buddy. For his posse, he took with him an investigating Federal agent by the name of Wild, a Deputy Marshall by the name of Bob Olinger whose own mother described him as a "natural born killer", and very same Barney Mason that chummed with Pat and Billy when the three rustled stock together.

His first attempt to ensnare his friend, involved pressuring the Kid's buddy Charlie Bowdre, threatening him with what would happen to his wife once he was swinging from a rope, and promising that he would arrange for a pardon for him once he told them where Billy was hiding. When that didn't work, they nabbed another Billy sympathizer at Fort Sumner, Juan Gallegos, and beat and tortured him until he reveled that the boys were staying at a nearby ranch. Garrett then bribed another man to tell the Kid that Garrett had left the area, ambushing the kid and his cohorts the moment they showed up in town. Drawing their own pistols and returning fire as they ran, they miraculously made their escape through a hailstorm of lead, all except for their compatriot Tom O'Folliard who still lay in the middle of the dusty Sumner street, clutching the agonizing stomach wound that would soon kill him.

An illustration fairly accurately portraying the cabin where Billy and crew were captured, taken from "The Authentic Life of Billy The Kid", a book that Pat Garrett commissioned his drinking buddy Ashmun Upson to write to cast him in a more generous light.

A bright moon and fresh blanket of snow made following the tracks of the Kid and his gang easy, and Garrett could already guess that they'd lead to the old Stinking Springs forage station where they'd often hung out together. Arriving a few hours before dawn, Pat positioned the others in places of concealment and waited. First to step out of the casita was Charlie Bowdre, gunned down as he carried a bag of feed to his horse. They also shot the horse, when they saw that Billy was trying to pull it inside for a safe mounting and getaway. A standoff resulted, broken only the next day when the Kid and his three pards smelled the bacon cooking in the posse's camp. It seems they had stockpiled plenty of guns and ammunition, but nothing to eat.

Sheriff Pat Garrett, Deputy John Poe &James Brent

Garrett jailed his young prisoners, and then proceeded to the capital of Santa Fe to claim the $500 reward. Governor Wallace was back on the East coast promoting the novel he had just completed, "Ben Hur", and the acting governor refused to make the payment due to a technicality. Territorial leaders – the so called Sante Fe Gang – were less hesitant, handing Pat a check for $1000 for helping rid them of these partisans of the political opposition. The Kid was tried for murder on March 28th, 1881 in Mesilla, one of the few courts where it was believed they could get a guilty verdict given Billy's wide spread support. Sentenced to be hung, Garrett moved him to the Lincoln County courthouse to await execution.

A silver plated watch housed in the wonderful Buffalo Bill Historical Center collection, inscribed from the "Grateful Citizens of Lincoln County, Sept. 1881," proof that Pat Garrett was often lauded and not always reviled.

Garrett was off conferring with politicos again when the Kid made his most daring escape, either retrieving a hidden Colt Peacemaker from beneath the outhouse privy or else seizing it from the holster of his guard, J. W. Bell, before shooting and killing him with it. Either way, it is certain that he was back upstairs and leaning out of the east window when his second guard, the abusive Bob Olinger, heard the shot and came running out of the saloon in his direction. Billy cradled in his arms the same 10 gauge shotgun that Olinger had often tormented him with, describing the effects it would have on the Kid if he cared to try and escape. Now the tables, or shotgun, were turned, and those imposing loads of .33 caliber balls ripped through the air and in the direction of Bob below. "Watch out," someone had yelled, "the Kid has killed Bell!" "Yes," Olinger muttered just before the balls ripped into his chest and cratered out his back, "and he has killed me too."

In the ensuing weeks, Garrett's reaction was said to be lackluster, even disinterested, as he continued to feel snubbed by the elites he supported. What's more, half the territory's Anglo population and nearly all of its Spanish speaking residents treated him like a pariah now for betraying his friends just to win a tin star. Under increasing pressure to act, Pat returned to Fort Sumner and resumed his heavy handed questioning of the locals. He soon found out that the Kid was staying with Pedro "Pete" Maxwell, the rancher who had years before fired him for dishonesty, and may have finally smiled as he set his trap. Sometime after midnight, Garrett snuck into Maxwell's compound and prepared to ambush Billy went he woke the next morning. According to Garrett, the Kid woke up hungry when it was still hours before dawn, grabbed his pistol with one hand and a large butcher knife with the other in order to cut some meat off the beef hanging in the kitchen. Sensing that there was someone lurking there in the shadows, he twice asked imploringly "Quien es? Quien es?", "who is it?" Claiming to fear for his life, Garrett answered The Kid's questions by firing his unholstered Colt revolver twice, the first round hitting him directly in the heart, and the second going wild. Billy The Kid, murderous outlaw and outright hero to the downtrodden and dispossessed, was likely dead before he hit the ground. April 18th, 1881.

While dead he was, eyewitness reports told a drastically different tale than Garrett's, describing him slipping early in the evening into the room of Billy's girlfriend – Maxwell's daughter Paulita – and tying her up. By their account, he employed not a handgun for the execution but his powerful Sharps buffalo rifle, a single .50 caliber shot entering his back directly below his left shoulder and smashing through his heart before exiting above the nipple.

One current officer of the law who has written about the event, insists that it is proper police protocol to fire first whenever believing oneself to be in mortal danger. Perhaps, but this misses the point that the Kid was apparently unarmed and given no chance to surrender, in what by all accounts – including Garrett's own – gives the appearance of a carefully executed, deadly ambush of an admittedly dangerous fugitive. They got out of there quickly, for the reason that the entire compound was by then awake and making a terrible mourning sound that the Sheriff feared could easily turn to mortal threats.

This illustration from Ashmun Upson's
The Authentic Life of Billy The Kid portrays
Garrett's fanciful version of his gunning
down of Billy the Kid in a pitch dark room
of the Maxwell hacienda... cast into doubt
by the absence of either a knife or revolver
at the scene, though few doubted the practicality
of ambushing the extremely dangerous Kid
when he was at his most vulnerable.

However it came down, the killing of the Kid brought little acclaim and much derision. The territorial government was again reluctant to pay him a reward. Seeking to cash in on his notoriety, Garrett asked a journalist and drinking buddy – Ashmun Upson – to help him write a book casting him in a more noble and courageous light. The result, *The Authentic Life of Billy The Kid, the Noted Desperado of The Southwest*

Whose Deeds of Daring and Blood Made His Name a Terror in New Mexico, Arizona, and Northern Mexico was rushed to print in 1882 but sales were dismal, in part due to Upson's whiskey-addled attempts at promotion, and partly because of Garrett's spreading disrepute, but neither was it helped any by their strapping it with a title that was a librarian's nightmare.

Merwin & Hulbert .38 revolver with Pat Garrett's name scrimshawed into its elephant ivory grips

Some sources say he ran again for Lincoln County Sheriff in 1882, others state with certainty that it was for Sheriff of Grant County that he ran for, but all agree that he lost by a landslide. The Rio Grande Republican newspaper dubbed Garrett "ungrateful and egotistical", after which Pat hunted down the suspected writer and clubbed him with his Colt. He then joined up with his old rustling partner Mason, and answered the Texas governor's call for a state funded militia to "protect" large ranching interests against what were believed to be the encroachments of a growing number of small independent ranchers. Garrett was again aligned with the rich and privileged, and an accomplice to the murders in captivity of many of the ranchers he'd helped to capture.

Garrett settled in Uvalde, Texas, for what were the most peaceful three and a half years of his life... peaceful enough to bore the heck out of him. In 1888, Garrett cofounded an investment company to divert water to farms in the Pecos Valley, but was soon pushed out by more savvy and better funded partners. Then in 1889, Garrett briefly returned to New Mexico to try one last time to win himself a sheriff's job, this time in Chaves County, but he was soundly trounced once again. His final reprise in law enforcement would be in 1896, when he sold his Uvalde property to accept a position as a private detective working for then Governor Thornton, and was then appointed Doña Ana County Sheriff, chasing the $2000 reward for the killer or killers of the controversial lawyer, Albert Fountain, and his nine year old son.

Fountain had just secured an indictment for rustling against ranch hands Oliver Lee, William McNew and James Gililland in Lincoln and was returning home to Las Cruces on a little used stretch of road through White Sands, when they were apparently ambushed and gunned down. All that was ever found was the bloodied buckboard they rode in.

With the primary suspects closely aligned with politician Fall, Garrett waited two years before presenting his evidence to the court. During that time he attempted to enlist in Col. Theodore Roosevelt's volunteers, the Rough Riders, an army unit whose ranks were being filled by rugged westerners from lawmen and cowboys to patriotic outlaws, but for whatever reason they wouldn't accept Garrett. Finally securing indictments in 1898, suspect McNew was fast arrested, while Lee and Gililland went into hiding. Garrett and five deputies surprised them on July 12th, but the two desperate men answered the attack with such heavy and accurate gunfire that Pat and his posse decided to beat a fast retreat, leaving behind deputy Kurt Kearney who lay face down and bled-out in the dirt. Lee and Gililland escaped to another judicial district where they surrendered, were tried on charges of first degree murder, exonerated and released.

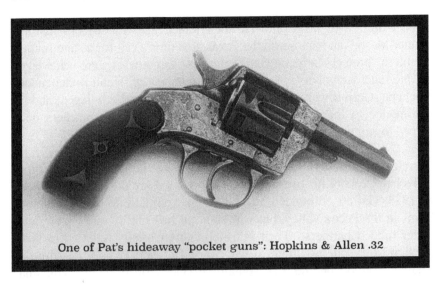

One of Pat's hideaway "pocket guns": Hopkins & Allen .32

By 1889 Garrett's drinking and gambling had gotten way out of hand, downing bitter cups filled at the hand of multiple disappointments. Never one to pay his debts, either to financial institutions or to friends, he was now at 50 years old facing the seizure of his New Mexico property over money owed to the Albuquerque Commerce Bank. Desperate for cash, his few influential friends took pity on him and petitioned the now President Theodore Roosevelt to appoint Pat as Customs Collector in El Paso, emphasizing Garrett's Wild West credentials and killing of Billy The Kid to the West-loving president. Within six months he faced court action over the way he had appraised cattle, and by 1903 a petition was circulated by irate importers and sent to the government to demand his removal. Multiple complaints of impropriety and corruption resulted in the U. S. Treasury Department launching an investigation, and the local Republican established lobbied hard to get rid of him. They resented that Pat had switched his allegiance from Democrat to Republican solely to qualify for the position, and they railed against his "Godless drinking", habitual gambling, and harsh criticism of the church. As far as the administration was concerned, the final straw came in 1905 when Garrett lied when introducing a buddy to the President at a Rough Rider reunion, billing the crooked owner of the Coney Island Bar – Bill Powers – as a respectable Texas cattleman. When it was pointed out to him, Roosevelt was incensed, and any thoughts of his defending Garrett's appointment were dashed for good.

By 1907, Pat was nearly debilitated by his constant gambling and public brawling, carrying out vendettas and abusing friends, abandoning his wife and children and moving in with a prostitute named "Mrs. Brown". His gambling and personal debts piling up, the ever more cantankerous Garrett moved to his remaining ranch. It was then that his main creditor, the rancher W.W. Cox, convinced Pat to give the five year lease to his employee, Jesse Wayne Brazel, unaware that he would be grazing despised goats instead of cattle. In 1908 he received an offer to buy the ranch, but only if he could break the lease with Brazel and remove the goats first, and Brazel refused. Ever so curiously, this cash offer was made by one of the most notorious of all bushwhackers, "Killin' Jim" Miller. And Miller's brother in law was Carl Adamson.

It was Adamson who drove the buckboard Garrett rode in, on what would be the final ride of his life. It wasn't long into their trip that they either accidentally or strategically came across Brazel. Ol' Pat hated Brazel's goats with a passion, but hated Brazel even more for screwing up the much needed sale by refusing to sell the lease back to him. Adamson later testified that there were only three of them there, that he had been standing next to Garrett engaged in the same bodily necessity, and that their backs were turned away from their nearby wagon when the fatal shots were fired. He told the same court of law that he had heard Garrett make increasingly ominous threats against Brazel, and that he had not been surprised to turn around and see the aggrieved Brazel holding a still smoking Colt revolver in his hand. Adamson further stated that Brazel then handed him the gun and voluntarily joined him on the wagon for the ride back to town to surrender. What's certain is that Brazel was soon released on a $10,000 bond provided by a cadre of ranchers headed by Cox, Brazel's employer who he professed complete loyalty to. The remarkable speed with which this money was collected, led to no small amount of suspicion thereabouts as to the clique's possible foreknowledge of or connivance in Garrett's elimination.

Brazel's trial opened on April 19th, 1909, with Albert B. Fall taking charge of the defense. His argument was a common one in the West, that he had made a preemptive strike against Garrett in the face of mortal danger, the same exact argument once made by Garrett to explain his murder of the Kid. Brazel claimed that Pat was trying to reach his always loaded shotgun, and that he had to shoot first in order to save his life.

Wayne Brazel, seated, gladly confessed to shooting Garrett after Pat had threatened him, but his confidence and the support he had waiting for him indicated to many there had been a conspiracy to finally get rid of the troublesome part-time lawman.

Indications that there was more to Garrett's killing – that others may have been in on it, or that it may not have even been Wayne Brazel who fired the fatal shots – are both numerous, and nearly overwhelming. To begin with, Adamson and Brazel left the body where it lay rather than bringing it to town as then would have been the custom, especially odd given that Adamson was supposedly Pat's friend. It was believed that Garrett's shotgun was still in the wagon and not in his hands, and that it was loaded with bird shot for quail rather than the buckshot it would be loaded with if he was expecting trouble. Brazel's revolver was never checked to see if rounds had recently been fired, and the accuracy of the killing shot was more indicative of a rifle shot. Empty brass rifle shells were found along with a fourth man's tracks at a spot overlooking the killing, politically influential people had quickly paid the cost of Bravel's bail and legal defense. Adamson, the only known eyewitness, was never called to the stand. No autopsy report has come to light to prove whether the bullet that killed him entered from the front or back, and the Prosecutor made only unenthusiastic assertions during the trial with only the briefest of examinations of the witnesses and the accused.

A number of writers agree with me that Pat was most likely taken down by an unseen rifleman hidden at the prearranged ambush site, very possibly Adamson or his brother-in-law Killin' Jim, and it's doubtful if Wayne Brazel fired at all. How is it that a peace loving young goat rancher who wasn't known for even carrying a gun, could cold bloodedly (and dare I point out, *accurately*) put a revolver round through the bullseye center of Garrett's hard head? If they really had been having a heated argument, as Adamson testified, why in heck would a seasoned, crusty, and lately downright paranoid man leave his weapon in the wagon and turn his back on Brazel to urinate? And what was it that made Brazel's supporters so certain of an acquittal, that they started getting together beef and a band for a dance party and barbecue weeks before a verdict was due to be handed down?

Some Western lawmen that I have studied have been revealed to be seemingly admirable beyond question, while most others proved a decidedly mortal mix of valuable qualities and lamentable traits, performing good and not so good deeds in the overall furtherance of public safety and order. Only one, Patrick F. Garrett, triggered what ended up a territory-wide celebration... by dying with his pride in his hand.

W. B. Masterson
Jan 19–1907

Chapter VIII

Bat Masterson

Integrity, Independence & Panache

The man who preferred to be called Bat, lawman and adventurer, lay slumped over in his chair. He'd died the way he wanted, with his "boots on" as that old saying goes, obstinately taking yet another stand against injustice. Still clutched tightly in Masterson's right hand, was one of the tools of his trade, in instrument with which he was known to be expert and dangerous... not the criminal humbling Colt .45 that he had so often in the past employed, but the New York made fountain pen with which he wrote his sometimes combative and characteristically opinion-filled newspaper columns, scratching away on sheets of pressed paper as automobiles and trolleys whooshed and clanged down the busy streets just outside. And the 68 year old man had died from a heart attack rather than a bullet, his final piece for the Morning Telegraph neatly arrayed on the desk before him.

The "ginks," he'd just written, "hold that because the rich man gets ice in the Summer and the poor man gets it in the Winter, things are breaking even for both... but I just don't see it that way." And there had been a lot of things he chose to see differently since moving from the West to the largest, most upscale city in the U.S.

It may have been three decades or so since this feisty pen-slinger had slung a gun on the streets of Dodge City, Kansas and Leadville, Colorado, yet he never stopped being known around the "Big Apple" for both his reported exploits out in the perennially alluring West. Even in his sixties, with whitened and receding hair, heavier build and slowed gait, he was in nearly all cases treated with deference as well as respect. He came across as "just a friendly ol' guy," as one reporter put it, "with one hell of a history."

As usual, the source of that so-often fanciful record were the many various literary and cinematic versions, from articles circulated during his time to Gene Barry's portrayal on TV in the 1960s. The lot were spiced up in every way possible in order to get the attention of potential readers and viewers, and to increase the circulation or viewership of the host papers or stations. And rather than simply making it all up from start, the majority of the authors and screenwriters got their juicy material from Masterson's many obliging buddies, always happy to fill in the gaps where truth leaves off, spinning some spectacular yarns intended to dismay and delude. As late as 1926, a Bat acquaintance by the name of Fred Sutton was quoted as saying the lawman was responsible for the planting of 37 evil doers in Dodge City's "Boot Hill." An earlier 1887 Kansas paper claimed he'd killed a man on his birthday every year since he was a boy. And it may have all started in 1881 in southern Colorado, when a gullible reporter from the New York Sun was directed by a certain Dr. W. Cockrell to the jauntily dressed friend he claimed had decapitated the murderers of his brother, and had killed a total of 26 men. Bat himself contributed to the fiction, through what he didn't say as much as through the responses he gave in that Sun interview.

"I've not killed as many men as supposed," was his cryptic reply, when quizzed by a Kansas City Journal correspondent in 1881. He confirmed his gunning down of his brother's assailants and then, apparently warming to subject, claimed to have killed seven others in a single gunfight, and then added that he'd been charged with murder four times but had always been found not guilty.

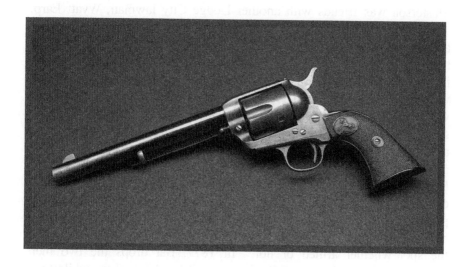

The Journal story, which would be reprinted in papers all around the country, ended with its author asserting "whether he has killed 26 men... cannot be positively ascertained... but that many men have fallen by his deadly revolver and rifle is an established fact," and concluded that here was "an illustration that the thrilling stories of life on the frontier are not always overdrawn."

"Overdrawn" would in fact be the nicest possible way to describe such chicanery. Bat may or may not have considered a benefit to claim such a fearsome reputation, but the intimidation value could well have made it easier for him to bring in alive every single lawbreaker he ever sets out after. That's right, *alive*... either sneaking up on them, "getting the drop," or more often negotiating a cooperative surrender. Bat certainly could have shortened the existence of a number of Indians when he and his company of fellow trappers were laid siege to.

It's likely that Masterson was the one to end the life of a certain highly jealous Sgt. King in an altercation at the Lady Gay bar in Sweetwater, Texas in 1876, even though even some reported the fatal shots came from the notorious Ben Thompson rather than Bat. And in April of 1878 he shot down two men after one of them had put a revolver slug through the belly of his brother Ed, a marshall of Dodge City at the time. This puts his possible lifetime record of men killed in a gunfight not at 38, or even 26, but at a more sober 2 or 3.

Masterson was friends with another Dodge City lawman, Wyatt Earp, and both would become exceptionally famous due largely to inflated accounts of their exploits. It was a late in life book of lies by Stuart Lake that cemented Earp as a cultural icon and shining knight, and the quoted interviews responsible for jump-starting Bat's considerable fame. Both were also were considered "sporting men", were great fans of boxing, wore badges for periods of their lives, were known to be exceedingly good with a gun, and by implication peed standing up... but that's about as far as the comparisons go.

Masterson bent or sidestepped the letter of the law on more than few occasions as we shall see, but unlike Earp, he never did so in an effort at personal enrichment. And while both men lost brothers to assailant's bullets, Earp tracked down the killers after the fact and executed them on the spot whether armed or not. In 1877, Bat drops the two men responsible for his brother Ed's death, but it he shoots them while they are armed and in the act. Earp was constantly fabricating in order to make himself look more important and less sinister than he was. Bat's motivation, on the other hand, seems to have been more to see how far he could stretch the truth and get away with it, in the time honored tradition of earthy mountain men and crusty westerners having great fun by making fools of slack jawed "flatlanders" and anxious rubes from the east.

Irrespective of the creative yarn spinning, Masterson's real life was irrefutably momentous and exciting. In 1871, at age 18, he left home to work as a buffalo hunter, and it was in the community of hunter's camps that he was introduced to the gambling and hard drinking that he would never quit. He was only 20 when he participated in the second battle of Adobe Walls, famous for the amazing 1,538 yard shot made by Billy Dixon with his .50 caliber Springfield, toppling a mounted Comanche medicine man and effectively ending the warriors' siege.

In early 1877, Bat got his first taste of law enforcement from then Dodge City Marshal, Larry Deager, a 300 pound bully of an officer who beat and then arrested him for daring to object to the manhandling of a local drunk. And his next taste came only a few months later, when he himself pinned on a badge, as the appointed Undersheriff of surrounding Ford County, Kansas.

One of Bat's brothers, Ed, was serving his first stint as city Marshall at the same time, a capable lawman who was well liked in the growing community. It was April 5th, 1878, when Ed was shot in the gut by an inebriated cowboy he was wanting to disarm. The shooter was Jack Wagner, jerking a revolver from concealment and letting loose at such close range that it set his shirt afire. Wagner's foreman, Alf Walker, then pulled his own hogleg and held the second officer, Nate Haywood, at bay. Hearing the shots from nearby, Undersheriff Bat raced to the scene within seconds, instantly engaging both gunmen from about 60 feet distance with his 5.5" barreled Colt .45. Four rounds were heard to go off one after the other, "as rapid as a gatling gun" as one over excited witness would later describe it to the press. The first of these pierced the offender, Jack, through the side, ventilating both lungs and dropping him to the ground. The second two caught Walker in the right arm and chest, effectively putting an end to the fight if not making things right. Walker survived and was released, only to die a couple years later from pneumonia related to the lung wound. Few were saddened by the death of the murderer, Wagner, but most of Dodge mourned the passage of kind and brave Ed Masterson.

Ed Masterson, center

A few credible historians have written asserted that it was a dying Ed, not Bat, who fired those four deadly shots, but the recent surfacing of original court records includes Bat's admission he was the one who so deftly pulled the trigger. Six months later, on October 5th, he demonstrated his firearms prowess once again by sending a .50 caliber slug from his own buffalo-bagging Sharps through the shoulder of an escaping Jim Kennedy, wanted for shooting a visiting songstress, Dora Hand, in an attempt to send the Dodge City mayor into permanent retirement instead.

Bat lost his position in the election of 1879, during which time he did his gunfighter friend, Ben Thompson, the honor of helping Ben's troublesome brother Billy escape a jail in Ogallala on a fast departing train. He pulled a similar trick only three years later while working as a gambler in Colorado, doing his sleezy pard Earp a favor by working out a scheme to keep the gunfighter Doc Holiday from being extradited to Arizona on charges relating to the shootout at O.K. Corral. In both cases, loyalty easily trumped bothersome legalities... something you just gotta like about the Old West!

Bat had followed Earp and any number of other boom town opportunists to Tombstone in 1880, but before the famed O.K. gunfight went down, he was called back to bleeding Kansas by a telegraph warning that the life of his surviving lawman brother, Jim, was threatened. Jim had recently been the latest Masterson to be picked to serve as a Dodge City peace officer. He'd also purchased a financial stake in the same Lady Gay Saloon in front of which brother Ed had been killed only a few years before. Within months he'd come into conflict with principle partner A.J. Peacock and A.J.'s combative, gun-totin' alcoholic bartender, Al Updegraff, precipitating the verbal threats that had spurred Bat's fast train back. Bat wasn't even getting along with Jim at this point, but that sure didn't keep him from immediately packing his guns and buying a ticket out.

Bat had barely gotten off the arriving train when he spotted the two antagonists and commanded them to halt. While it remains unclear who fired the first shot, rounds were almost immediately sent sailing in both directions over the Santa Fe Railroad tracks, with a few uninvolved and uninformed bystanders on both sides evidently joining in the target shooting just for the fun of it. Peacock and Updegraff fired from around the corners of the Dodge City jailhouse, their misses penetrating the walls and emptying out the patrons of McCarty's Drugstore and the famed Long Branch Saloon. Bat's slugs were better placed, sending splinters into his adversaries eyes with preliminary shots, and then airmailing one through Al Updegraff's lung before pausing to reload.

Ab Webster, Dodge City's current mayor, took advantage of the temporary lull to hurry and place Bat under arrest, emphasizing his mayoral authority with an American made, Fox brand, double barreled 12 gauge shotgun. Once assured by Webster that his brother Jim was alive and well, Bat was checked in to the very jail that he'd just shot up. Tough ol' Al recovered quickly, and a sympathetic or perhaps star-struck judge found Bat guilty only of "reckless firing of a gun" and letting him go after paying an $8 fine. It would prove to be the last gunfight that Bat Masterson ever fought.

That Masterson was a crack shot, there can be no doubt. Early on, it seems he was the one to put the hurt on the enraged Sgt. King at close quarters, even though King had already "started the ball rolling." Bat's deciding shot with his 12 pound Sharps rifle was taken offhand, standing up, and at a fast moving target. And when the hammer dropped in '78, he put all four fired rounds into Ed's attackers before either could take aim and fire at him... while unsteady from being out of breath!

It was not accuracy alone that settled fights in his favor, of course, but the quality that Bat later described as a writer: deliberation. From his oft quoted book Human Life: "Courage to step out and fight to the death with a pistol is but one of three qualities a man must possess in order to last very long in this hazardous business. Courage is of little use to a man who essays to arbitrate a difference with the pistol if he is inexperienced in the use of the weapon he is going to use. Then again he may possess both the courage and the experience and still fail if he lacks deliberation."

Bat flirted with running various Colorado businesses while taking up the art of writing with the same deliberateness he had earlier given to gun handling and shooting. He took particular pleasure in writing about two especially combative contests, politics and boxing, and made many enemies as well as friends in the process of railing against the fraud so common to both. It was over what he believed to be a fixed fight in Denver, that he finally departed the West for the East and never looked back again. His job at the Telegraph met his needs nicely, in an environment where he could wear his fanciest suits and derby hats without looking out of place.

What struck me in reading a number of Bat's newspaper columns, was how contemporary his comments sound even though penned nearly a hundred years ago. When he says "Clerical humbugs and sordid politicians are certainly giving the decent, liberty-loving people of this country a lively run for their existence," he could be talking about today. And it wouldn't be unusual to walk into any bar or café in North America and hear people echoing Masterson quotes such as: "When a man becomes so throughly disgusted with his own country that he wants to leave it and never return, conditions are certainly in a deplorable state." Or his "Political liberty has become a ghastly joke and the end is nowhere in sight." Or even "The time is not far distant when red-blooded men will get guns and use them, too. They'll either have to do that or turn the country over to the modern witch-burners... [for] hypocrisy, rascality and cowardice have supplanted liberty, bravery and integrity."

Masterson could opine about such matters without fear of being branded a hypocrite or poseur, given that he comes as close as any lawman to exemplifying both integrity and independence. For the most part, he functioned like a true Peace Officer in the best sense of the term, and did it in resplendent style just as a character of the Western imagination should. And yet, the fellow who once rejected his birth name, Bartholomew, because it sounded too formal and civilized, seems to have never suffered any great nostalgia for the frontier he helped to transform. He was happy to move someplace where the streets were cleaned, intellect valued, and good theater always close at hand. "To hell with the West," he once went so far as to say, when asked for the umpteenth time if he was aching to go back. He nonetheless remained a true Westerner in the attitude he displayed and approach he preferred.

"The man who will back up what he says with a fight if necessary is to be respected," he wrote, in anything but New York diction, "while the one who assails character and then seeks refuge behind the law deserves nothing but contempt."

Such frontier values do not preclude allowing the rube to look the fool, however, and Bat's later in life pranks included buying old Colts from nearby pawn shops, adding suggestive notches, and selling them for a mint to people as the "one" he carried in the old days wearing a badge. Curiously, one of these foolhardy buyers was the same Fred Sutton who set the number of Bat's kills at 38.

The line between inspiring mythos and despicable lie, between suggestion and fact, fiction and history can be a fine one. With only the slightest of hints, all too many of us are quick to imagine what it is we long to see or hear... an advantage easily exploited by writers as well as stage magicians, manipulative politicians and survival-minded ex-gunfighters.

A telling case in point occurred in the lobby of the Waldorf-Astoria hotel in June of 1906, when an aging Bat confronted a Texas book publisher and his reputed to be famous author. The author, calling himself Col. Dick Plunkett, had been showing off a hog-leg Colt with more notches carved into it than on any Masterson prepped and sold gun, telling tales of daring-do to an assembled crowd while lambasting Bat as a fraud and a phony. As might be expected, an indignant Bat soon made his appearance on the scene, drawing his big fist back and duly knocked the offending editor to the hard marble floor. Turning to face the armed Plunkett, he thrust his gun hand into his pocket, reportedly prompting someone to yell "Lookout, Bat's going to flash his cannon!" The crowded room then emptied out quicker than anyone could have believed possible, with the supposed "Colonel" among the first pilgrims out the door.

Such antics were of course frowned upon in the city, even back then, and the policemen who escorted Masterson outside also wanted to see the heat he was carrying. Bat smiled, and pulled out for the officers what was an apparently amply intimidating silver cigarette case. Based on his reputation, people expected him to have been packing and ready to use his gun, so that is what they pictured. As in nearly all cases of larger than life personas – lawmen or not – it ain't necessarily facts that determine how people react, but rather, what we've come to believe.

Chapter IX

George Scarborough

He Shot First & Asked Questions Later

"I'd rather run men than cattle."
-George Scarborough, 1893 June

An expression we often hear bandied about, "Shoot first, ask questions later" seems to have enigmatic origins that may or may not be historic. We hear it applied to everything from inner city policemen who fire on suspects without warning, to politicians who speak before they think. What we most associate it with, however, is the Old West, where men on both sides of the law often chose preemptive action over anything resembling a

Hollywood version of fair play. One man who epitomized this approach was the part time lawman, part time bounty hunter whom detractors called "Old Scarbrow."

And contrary to what Hollywood productions might lead us to believe, there were really very few genuine bounty hunters – private sleuths working to apprehend fugitives without the benefit of the law or the protective cover of a tin star – in the Old West. Bounties were generally far too low, and the chances of death much too high, to make it an appealing career choice for many. There were a number of badge-wearing manhunters, however, who augmented their truly pitiful deputy's or marshall's wages by cashing in on the rewards offered for various notable miscreants. The honorable triumvirate of Heck Thomas, Chris Madsen and Bill Tilgham readily come to mind, as does the name of George Scarborough. Scarborough's doggedness on the trail and courage in a fight made him a dangerous man to have on one's tail. When it came time to enlist help for hunting down and seeking to capture some of the most desperate of Southwestern *desperadoes*, it was often to Scarborough that the greatly respected officer Jeff Milton turned, even though he considered him just a mite too eager to drop a hammer and take a life, because as Milton put it, George "aint afraid of no man."

The few historians and aficionados who have heard of Scarborough usually know him only as the man who killed the killer of John Wesley Hardin. It was Scarborough, after all, ended the life of "Uncle" John Selman, while Selman was awaiting a second trial for having sensibly if cowardly shot the famed shootist Hardin in the back of the head in the Acme Saloon in El Paso, Texas, August 18th, 1895. But his always busy career as a lawman began ten years earlier when he was elected Sheriff of Jones County, Texas, and didn't culminate until his life ended in 1900, after suffering a gunshot wound in the line of duty.

George Adolphus Scarborough was born October 2nd, 1859, in Natchitoches Parish, Louisiana, just prior to the War Between The States, his childhood partly spent in Texas with his family trying to avoid the rampant race riots then raging in the Colfax area near new Orleans, and partly spent back in Louisiana as his father sought to dodge the Indian raids on the increase in southern *Tejas* at that time. George's early work was as a cowboy, and reports that he rustled his share of cattle could have either been the defaming of a well behaved man by disgruntled associates and onlookers, or else honest indications that the future officer once had a hand in some of the very same activities that he later arrested others for doing. One way or the other, he most certainly developed a depth of familiarity with the outlaws of the region and their ways that would serve him well once later assigned to their pursuit. And Scarborough's reputation for "shooting first and asking questions later" are evidenced in the fact that he was tried three times for murder in a court of law while wearing a badge. On the other hand, he was, in the end, exonerated each of those three times, including by juries who could as easily held him to task.

It was in Jones County during his very first term as a lawman that an event happened which I tend to believe shaped his subsequent hard attitude, implacable manhunts and seemingly unhesitant applications of effectively directed violence. It was December 21st, 1885, one year before Winchester Firearms Company revolutionized the repeating rifle by releasing their John Browning designed Model 1886 lever action, and only three years following the famed "Gunfight at the O.K. Corral." Scarborough had corralled a pair of young, hard case robbers A.B. "Add" Cannon and Joseph Brown, and then turned them over to the care of his jailer, William C. Glazner. He'd hired the inexperienced Bill in part because of how much the father of six kids needed the job and income, and no doubt felt some responsibility for what followed. Asked for cigarette papers, the kindly Glazner turned his back on an underwear clad Cannon long enough to be struck on the head with an iron bar he'd concealed in a towel, and was then repeatedly clubbed until bleeding and unconscious. Unable to quickly find the keys to doors, Add snatched the pistol from the jailer's holster and made his exit through a glass transom hinged above the office door.

Scarborough's unsuccessful attempts to track down the killer Cannon – both in the days following the murder of his jailer, and for those many years after – remained a sore spot for him for the rest of his life. If he was indeed "trigger happy" it was apparently not out of a blood lust or even rancor so much as lead sent downrange in the course of never doing what Glazner had, and never letting another man get "the drop" on him. If there was to be any killings, he seems to have decided, he would be sure to be at the giving end rather than the receiving.

George Scarborough with Deputies

This fact was first borne out not long after, on October 15th, 1887, in a drinking establishment called the Q.T. or "Road To Ruin Saloon." According to one tale, Sheriff Scarborough was at the bar facing the mirror when he saw a man he had been having trouble with, A.J. Williams, walk into the saloon behind him and draw his gun, at which point George is said to have managed to draw, wheel around and fire a fatal round all before Williams had time to pull the trigger. An official hearing into the shooting required only 5 minutes to determine it "the most clearest case of justifiable homicide we ever saw" in spite of few witness claiming to have seen anything at all. The speed of the verdict in favor of their lawman was as much as anything an indictment of the deceased, with Williams generally considered a bad man worth removing. Even Mrs. Williams cast a harsh vote, when she supposedly ran up to the startled Sheriff and told him not bother apologizing for dosing her husband with lead. "He was hardly ever home anyway, and we lived in fear when he was."

Scarborough's next appointment was as Deputy Federal Marshall under his old acquaintance Dick Ware, making him responsible for all the thinly populated desert counties between the Pecos and Rio Grande Rivers, South and East of El Paso where he was headquartered. His primary activities in this position were the arrest of smugglers, much as the Border Patrol is enlisted to do today, and he was known to confront (some said "shake down") the suppliers of illegal alcohol and opium, and to interdict the much despised illegal aliens then said to be pouring in over a too-porous border with Mexico... not Mexicans, mind you, but undocumented Chinese immigrants believed to be taking all the low wage jobs from American

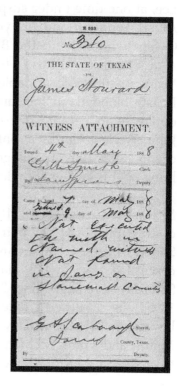

citizens. George's prejudice against other races is well reported, including an incident where he viscously beat up a black man for daring to sit at a table where there were whites, but the anti-Chinese sentiment in particular was typical of rather than exceptional in his time, a fervor reflected in the many loads of "Celestials" that Scarborough arrested.

El Paso in the years he served there, 1891 through 1896, was considered the last mecca for gamblers, "soiled doves" of the sex trade and professional gamblers, and a last bastion of the "Wild West," even as the country overall was rushing headlong into what it considered to be the modern age. Taking residence within the city's "sporting" milieu were some of the most resected or feared of gunmen including: John Wesley Hardin, freshly out of prison with a law degree but once the most deadly man alive. Hardin's violent brother in law, Mannie Clements. John Selman, who would shoot Hardin in the back of the head. "Fighting" Tom Tucker, Bud Frazer, and Billy the Kid's killer, Pat Garrett. Oliver Lee, at one time under suspicion of murdering the politician Col. Albert Fountain and his young son Henry. Commodore Perry Owens who shot up the Blevins gang in Southeastern Arizona.

And Martin M'Rose (or Mroz), a minor formidable Polish blooded rustler and outlaw who became one of John Wesley Hardin's only clients after the gunslinger hung out his lawyer shingle.

Jefferson Davis Milton

M'Rose earned the distinction of being Scarborough's second confirmed kill, when late Saturday evening, June 29, 1895, he enlisted fellow lawmen Jeff (Jefferson Davis) Milton and Frank McMahon to assist in Martin's arrest.

M'Rose had taken refuge south of the border to avoid criminal charges in the U.S., but was fairly fuming to hear his lawyer Hardin was "making hay" with his wife Beulah. It was said of Scarborough that he "never met a reward he didn't like," and it was to win the money offered for his capture that George ostensibly tricked Martin into following him across the Mexican Railway Bridge over the Rio Grande and to an area where a field of tall sunflowers concealed McMahon and Milton.

M'Rose reportedly toyed with his Colt SAA .45 as they proceeded down the tracks, one with a bobbed 2" barrel that had been given him by his friend Vic Queen.

At a prearranged signal from Scarborough the men stood up and all three drew down on M'Rose. As before, George would later assert that another badman had cocked a pointed a gun at him first, and that he was somehow able to draw and fire his weapon faster than Martin could squeeze the trigger of his already aimed Colt.

M'Rose Sawed-Off Colt

Undisputed by his fellow lawmen was the fact that it was George who fired first, with Milton opening up with a shotgun and McMahon with a rifle after M'Rose gamely rose up from the ground with Queen's large frame belly gun in his hand. If it was for the official reward rather for a roll of money some later said Scarborough lifted off the body, then it must have proven a fiscal disappointment since the reward was only for the fugitive's safe return and not the proverbial "Dead or Alive."

The coroner would report "seven penetrative wounds" including two through the heart and six or seven buckshot wounds to the left arm, with the initial and fatal round having been Scarborough's, a discharge of weapons that the investigators considered to be a "lawful discharge of duties." It was then that the tide of fickle public opinion began to tun on him, his deceptiveness at getting M'Rose to cross the bridge being considered distasteful at best by a populous rooted in the historic past and holding fast to old time concepts of chivalry and honor.

It was George Scarborough's next killing, however, that would become the one for which he'd become best known. "Uncle" John Selman had for years been pursued by various law enforcement authorities for assorted crimes including murder, cattle rustling and rape, though the courts were never able to compile enough evidence to take him to trial. In spite of or in part because of his unsavory reputation, he had managed to find enough support among the "sporting crowd" of El Paso to be elected as the Constable for Precinct 1 in the Autumn of 1892. Only three years later, on August 19th, 1895, he earned everlasting infamy with the murder of John Wesley Hardin.

Selman and Hardin had played several hands of poker together in the Acme Saloon, with Selman leaving and returning more than once. Hardin was standing up at the bar with his back to the doors, throwing dice with a hero worshipping neighborhood grocer named Harry Brown, when – just as the hands of the barroom clock reached for the eleven o'clock hour – old Uncle John stepped back through the saloon doors and put a .45 slug through the back of John Wesley's head. Selman fired three more shots into the body as it fell, before exiting the building with his grown son. He was quickly arrested and charged with murder, with Justice of The Peace Howe finding that "on the 19th day of August, one John Selman of his malice aforethought... did shoot the deceased with a revolver... from the effects of which the deceased died." Selman's version was that Hardin saw him in the mirror and then commenced to draw his gun first, though hardly anyone really believed that. The jury, however, decided they were happy enough to be rid of Hardin regardless of the circumstances of his death. "Had he been shot from in front," the jury report stated, "we would call it excellent marksmanship. As he was shot from behind, we must call it excellent judgement."

It could well have been the way that Hardin was killed, with complete lack of warning, that encouraged Scarborough's already quick hand, when on April 5th, 1896, he slammed the deadly Uncle John to the ground with four rounds from his personal Colt. The two men had stepped out of the Wigwam Saloon and into the near blackness of the alley behind, ostensibly to discuss the repatriation of Selman's son from the Juarez jail where he was being charged with kidnapping

Ornery
John Selman

for having eloped there with a young girl. Whatever previous relationship the men may have had, it seems clear they were never friends, though the exact reason for the shooting may never be determined. According to a statement made by Selman on his deathbed, Scarborough had for no cause jerked his gun and shot him in the back of the neck, before pumping three more rounds into him as he went down. George's version is quite different, of course, claiming that Uncle John had been toying with his weapon and acting threateningly, and that one more time he had simply yanked his firearm faster than a normal human could shoot, and thus managed to be the one administering the wounds rather the man nursing them.

Site of Wigwam Saloon

To confuse matters, Selman's revolver came up missing at the crime scene, supposedly snatched up from the ground by an opportunistic member of the crowd that quickly formed, but leading to multiple theories, including one put forward by Selman's Scarborough-hating friends, that it had been secretly lifted from his holster prior to them stepping outdoors to talk. It is patently absurd to think a hardened and experienced gunman like Uncle John would ever allow their gun to be snitched, or that he could possibly have been drunk enough not to have felt the absence of over three pounds of much beloved iron. But just as absurd, is Scarborough's assertion that he was able to sense Selman preparing to shoot him, and still get off four shots before his opponent could get off any. The round to the back of Selman's neck is reminiscent of his own recent shooting of Hardin, leading this writer to believe George was taking into account his methods, concluding that preemptive

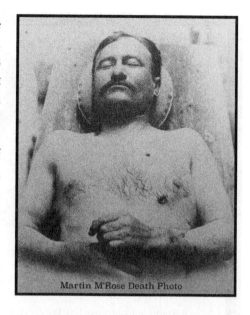
Martin M'Rose Death Photo

offense could indeed be the best defense. A jury seemed to support that idea, acquitting George of the expected murder charges even as he still faced trial for the leaden ventilation of M'Rose.

It was at this time, in 1897, that Jeff Milton looked up Scarborough and requested his assistance pursuing and capturing an effective crew of train robbers named after the card game "High Fives." George was in need of money and in between jobs, and there were healthy rewards being offered by the train companies for these and other associates of what would go down in history as the Black Jack gangs. George worked undercover gathering information for awhile, and then joined Milton and the rest of a posse corralling several alleged gang members, one of whom stated they were about to be shot down by the lawmen when posse-man Cipriano Baca intervened. Milton says that shortly afterwards, George suggested to him that they gun down Black Jack Ketchum cohort John Cush rather than go to the trouble of arresting him, with Milton objecting they couldn't just kill a man in cold blood. But even with all the reservations that Jeff had, he considered Scarborough one of the few he could count on to be there when the going got tough.

by Jesse Wolf Hardin

A Study in Contrasts: Jeff Milton (left) with George Scarborough

So as to be sure of getting the rewards and not having to share any of them, Scarborough stepped away from his work as a range detective and Milton took leave from his position as messenger guard with Wells, Fargo & Company. One of the most felonious of the Black Jack remnants was train robber and all around *hombre* Bronco Bill Walters, and he became their first target and focus. Hiring the services of Apache trackers, the two now self employed bounty hunters caught up with Walters on July 30, 1897, spreading out around a remote cow camp and setting their trap. Bill rode right up to where Scarborough stood before realizing who he was. George unhesitatingly cut loose with his fast barking Winchester 1886 rifle, already putting four holes in the gregarious bandit before Milton made it onto the scene. Bill fell from his horse with blood spurting from his mouth, just as incoming rounds from over 300 yards away suddenly started slamming into the ground nearby. In response, Scarborough found himself a good rest for his rifle and carefully returned fire, causing Bronco Bill associate Red Pippin to hightail it over the nearest ridge, and smashing Kid Johnson's hips with what would prove to be a painful and fatal wound.

With the breakup of the gangs and dissipation of rewards, Milton went back to distinguished career with Wells Fargo, and Scarborough resumed working for the Southwest's cattle grower's associations. Even though he was expensive, they considered him the "cheapest and best insurance" against cattle loss. They would remain his favored employers, in fact, as they paid well and gave their gunmen free rein, willingly overlooking what the prosperous cattlemen often considered the problematic "fine points" of the law. 1900 marked the end of a century, the beginning of the end of the once limitless frontier and the onset of more urbane ways, yet times still found Scarborough's gun toting services in high demand. It was profitable, exciting, and somehow satisfying, this hunting down and handcuffing or eliminating of dangerous adversaries. The last such cattle thieves he would "match up with" were a bunch whose trail led up into the Chiricahua Mountains of SE Arizona, and to a place called Triangle Springs that would ever after be known as Outlaw Springs instead.

Leading the way for Scarborough was cattlemen's agent Walt Birchfield, who later told his story to reporters. According to Birchfield, they rode up to within 75 yards of the rustlers' camp before dismounting and getting into firing positions. "There's no use to call on them to surrender," George characteristically remarked before sending three or four rifle rounds their way, apparently without effect. The outlaws moved to cover from 200 to 350 yards distance, with Scarborough and Birchfield remounting their horses in order to circle to a better position themselves. They had ridden only a short ways before Walt says he heard a "pop like hitting a rock" as a .30 caliber steel jacketed bullet crashed into George's right leg, passing through both the saddle and blanket before lodging just under the skin of his horse. Times had indeed changed, as both Scarborough and his assailant fired the newfangled .30-40 Krag rounds, smokeless cartridges with much greater accuracy and range then anything before. More bullets continued to strike all around them. As Birchfield tells it:

"...when my horse got loose and ran off with my Winchester, I ran to (George's) horse and got his gun." He grabbed his cartridge belt off of him, too, since he needed .30-40s and all he had on him were his own .30-30s. "The lead would hit the rocks and bust, and would sound almost as loud as when shot out of a gun. The splattering lead cut my head and arms."

The inert Scarborough regained consciousness at that moment, calling out to Walt who then crawled over and to heard him say "I'm dying, I am no more" as he covered him with his coat and then crawled off in the direction of help. The old manhunter proved he wasn't ready to "cash in his chips" yet, however, remaining conscious the long night and day until Birchfield got back with a buckboard to retrieve him. Back at the family home, a Dr. Swope anesthetized Scarborough and fished out as many bone fragments from his shattered leg as he could. He never came out of it, and died at 2 the next morning, April 5th. Afterwards, Jeff Milton would grill the doctors about his death, and discovered that in the end it was medical malpractice and chloroform that stopped his heart, and not any of the bullets that were ever sent his way.

There are many who feel a need to tell only a partial story, to whitewash facts or sanitize the image of historical characters in order to be able to celebrate their lives. For them, it is necessary to discount reports of George Scarborough's own stretching of the law, and to justify his every fatal shooting in the interest of an unblemished hero. Others might identify what they believe to be his indiscretions, writing him off as a bushwhacker, or demonizing him for the often unannounced and often liberal exercise of his eager trigger finger. But like any man or woman, we had in him elements of both good and bad. He seemed happy to cut down men without giving them a chance, rather than chance being shot himself. But he also once refrained from shooting an old man who had mistakenly sent a slow moving .38 slug through his cheek.

It bears repeating, that the Old West – and life itself – was never so clear cut as some would have it. It was often only a disproportionately heavy application of power and the threat or actuality of violence that pulled in the reins on rampant criminal depredations, and the men who wielded that power were almost without exception a complex mix of good and bad, commendable and lamentable. Their every violent act was set in a complicated, multi-factional and political context that we can only begin to imagine from our seats of comfort over a hundred years after the fact. And each violent act would have a nearly equal number of folks vociferously applauding it as condemning it. Because a shooting or hanging was done under the auspices of the law doesn't mean it was – or is – always just. Not by any means! But neither is a deadly ambush without warning.

It is nonetheless perhaps misleading to call George Scarborough a "shoot first and ask questions later" guy.

As far as we know, he didn't have many questions.

Scarborough's Pearl-handled Colt SA

Chapter X

Bear River Smith

Hard Fists, Jovial Demeanor, & Gritty Determination

In 1871, when James Butler "Wild Bill" Hickok took over the job of Marshal of that rough and tumble cowtown, Abilene, he was being hired to take over for the recently murdered lawman "Bear River" Tom Smith. Both were tall, handsome and unarguably courageous, with large expressive hands and drooping frontier mustaches... and yet, the two could not have been much less alike when it came to temperament and style.

Bill was a killer known to be moody with periods of sullen withdrawal, characteristically wary and suspicious, quick to pull his sidearms and obsessive about making sure he had the advantage and got "the drop" on any potentially dangerous hombres. He appeared calm and unflustered in most situations, and drew and fired his favored Navy Colts with more sureness than speed. Ol' "Bear River", on the other hand, was said to be generally gregarious and trusting, giving little consideration to planning and strategy when rushing into a situation where he might be needed. Smith seldom ever drew his revolvers, and most strikingly – if you'll forgive my pun – preferred to disable any uncooperative miscreants with his bare fists instead. His sending confrontational drunks to jail with a black eye and bruises instead of to an early grave, was said by some to be due to his caring heart, while others remarked it was more a matter of *huevos* that dragged on the ground.

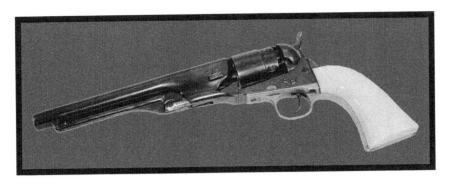

Little is known of the red headed Smith from the time of his 1830 birth somewhere in New York, until he left that state for the West as a workman helping to construct the Union Pacific railroad. Legend has it that he was a professional middleweight boxer and served at least briefly as a NYC policeman, although no evidence exists as to either. It's compelling to imagine him a cop from the time he's teethed, transferring his Rocky-like pugilistic skills from the bloodied bare-knuckle rings of eastern gentlemen's clubs to the frontier of cowboys, Indians and gunslingers. Even more intriguingly, it is said that he may have accidentally shot and killed a 14 year old boy in the line of duty, and then either jumped bail or was trying to get as far away as possible from the site and the act for which he was ashamed... just as Wild Bill would do some years later after mistakenly putting a slug through the chest his own deputy and friend. If so, it could help explain Tom's future reluctance to resort to arms, and his fervent promotion of and enforcement of widely unpopular gun control laws.

It seems Smith was not yet so reluctant when, in 1868, the first documented accounts of him appear. The incident that earned Tom his name occurred the ad hoc labor camp of Bear River, Wyoming, where rough and rowdy workers topped off days of hard labor with drinking, whoring, brawling and impromptu indoor target shooting. According to legend, again, the "town's" authorities had either arrested or hung a troublesome railroad worker, resulting in a retaliatory attack on the town by his track-laying buddies. Smith is claimed to have stood with guns drawn between the town citizens and angry workers, keeping the peace until military troops from Fort Bridger showed up to relieve him and lay down some good old fashioned martial law.

Bear River City, Wyoming

The more likely scenario, according to the few contemporary reports, is that Smith was part a growing crowd of laborers demanding the release of some fellow workers who were being held by self appointed "town" vindicators, no more than vigilantes in reality, enforcers of a version of peace, morality and ultimately mercantilism that apparently didn't sit so well with the unruly and party minded railroaders. The townsmen quickly switched from dishing out punishment to hunkering down in a log cabin, firing out of the windows into the milling men amassed outside. One of these bullets struck a friend of Smith's, causing him to jerk his pistol and charge the fort, and another is said to have brought him down and nearly killed him.

Whatever happened, he was certainly well enough two years later to apply for the position of Marshal of Abilene, a cowtown where herders not much different than his railroad chums were regularly tearing things up. His job this time, however, was not to defend the rabble's freedoms but to tighten the cinch on them and tame their rowdy ways. At first, the town councilmen passed his application over in favor of importing a supposedly heavily decorated ex-Cavalryman, but Abilene's mayor, Theodore C. Henry, was desperate for someone that could go head to head with hard-headed Texas drovers. The councilmen had second thoughts, after the aforementioned rough rider took the bullet scars in the "No Guns Allowed" sign at the edge of town as encouragement to ride on the other way.

Mayor Henry swore Bear River in as Abilene's Chief of Police on Saturday, June 4th of 1870, for a not too princely sum of $150 a month. The Chief was also the only policeman, and responsibility for keep things calm would rest on a single man. Whatever good a handgun might ever have done for him, in his first week on the job Tom Smith took it upon himself to enforce a languishing ordinance against toting firearms in town. First to rise to the test was a local hulk of man by the name of "Big Hank" Hawkins. His response to Tom's mild mannered requests to disarm, was to rest a hand on his holstered handgun and start to yell profanities in the Marshal's face. A swift right cross caught him on the temple, putting an end to his admonitions and dropping him to the ground, with Smith lifting Hawkin's gun from its leather as he folded and fell. When he came to, Smith ordered him to get out of town and never come back, a suggestion that his now suggestible opponent readily took.

Only a few days later, Big Hank's pard, "Wyoming Frank" decided to defend the interests of the sporting crowd by goading the Marshal into a gunfight. Frank was brave enough, locating Smith in one of the saloons, getting in his face and calling him out, and stepping rearwards to make room for his draw. But with each step that he took backwards, Smith took just as large a step forward until the two men were at the swinging doors, still nearly nose to nose. As the doors flew open, a left-right combination put out Frank's lights, enabling Bear River to take his time relieving his adversary of his weapon. Seeing what had gone down, other now slightly sobered patrons suddenly began to pull sidearms out of pockets and purses, from boot tops and out from under coats where they'd been artfully concealed, hurrying to offer them up to the bodacious Marshal. "Just check 'em with the bartender, boys, so's you can pick 'em up on your way out of town," he is reported to have said, before following after Frank as he was carried unconscious to the waiting calaboose. Upon waking up, apparently the same kind advice was given to Wyoming Frank as had been rendered to his pard, and it seems that he, too, found it to be good and actionable advice.

Then in June of 1870, Smith was called to investigate the theft of of large number of Abilene horses by some no-gooders led by one "Buckskin Bill". Tom followed their trail hundreds of miles north and out of state, to a place called Pawnee City where Bill had managed to sell the majority of the filched steeds. It was a hot and dusty July afternoon, when Smith rode his grey dappled gelding, Silverheels, slowly through the town, watching in all directions for the thieves, and taking note of the location of any Kansas steeds. Irate objections by a few of their new owners regarding the animals removal, were apparently overruled by the mere intimation of violence at the hands of the steely eyed man from the south.

Hearing of the pursuit, Buckskin Bill conveniently got himself thrown into jail in his hometown of Brownville on what may have been a bogus charge at the behest of his locally influential father. Smith rode back to Abilene with more than a dozen of the recovered horses herding in front of him, much to the bemusement of the townsfolk watching and waving from the raised wooden boardwalks. It's not recorded if Bear River either motioned or shouted greetings to them in return, or if perhaps only a hint of satisfaction was betrayed by the up-curled edges of his lips beneath their mustache curtain. A grateful city rewarded Bear River with a matching pair of Colt's percussion revolvers featuring polished elephant ivory handles, trophies that he proudly wore from then on yet supposedly hardly ever unsheathed.

The dauntless Smith had been on the job for less than five momentous months, when in November of '70 he took a part time deputy named Jim McDonald with him on a trip 12 miles outside of town to arrest a farmer, Andrew McConnell, on a charge of murder. McDonald was known to be uncomfortable with firearms, and when it came to *huevos*, he was considered to walk a little light... yet for whatever unknown reasons, it was nonetheless he who was enlisted to join in what would prove a fateful adventure.

Tom Smith, Abilene Marshal

As the two approached McConnell's farmhouse they noticed a friend of McConnell's, Moses Miles, standing guard in front of the door with a rifle cradled at his side. Smith instructed Deputy McDonald to cover

Miles, as the Marshal strode straight into the house and McConnell's waiting guns. Shots were fired, some of which may or may not have wounded the Marshal, and then the two of them closed distance and began to grapple. Upon hearing the shots, Miles raised his Winchester towards the deputy and snapped the hammer, but the rifle either misfired or its chamber was empty, making him temporarily vulnerable to an attack. Instead of seizing the opportunity, however, the Deputy Jim panicked and leapt on his horse for a speedy getaway, even as the Marshal and McConnell rolled out the door in a macabre death hug from which only one would ever rise. With a herculean effort, Tom had managed to flip his quarry over and slap some handcuffs on him, just as a remorseless Moses hit him over the head with the butt of his unfired rifle. Grabbing a nearby axe, he then struck a second blow that nearly took the head off of the courageous but incautious Smith.

The grateful and bereaved citizens of Abilene laid Bear River Tom Smith on a hill with a wooden marker, but in 1904 the remains of Bear River were exhumed and transferred to Abilene Cemetery beneath a sizable granite boulder with a bronze plaque reading: "Thomas J Smith, Marshal of Abilene, 1870. Died a Martyr To Duty Nov. 2, 1870. A Fearless Hero Of Frontier Days Who In The Cowboy Chaos Established The Supremacy Of Law." Decades later, the U.S. President Dwight D. Eisenhower said of his hero: "According to the legends of my hometown he was anything but dull. While he almost never carried a pistol he... subdued the lawless by the force of his personality and his tremendous capability as an athlete. One blow of his fist was apparently enough to knock out the ordinary 'tough' cowboy. He was murdered by treachery."

Tom Smith might have done better by both picking a different deputy than Jim McDonald, and walking in with a rifle or shotgun already cocked and leveled. The growing ambivalence of this brave badge wearer regarding the employment of firearms, may in fact have cost him his life.

We know that Pat Garrett liked to make arrests from ambush, Wild Bill and Wyatt Earp both preferred to "buffalo" any lawbreakers or contenders, smacking them atop the head with the barrel of a revolver. But it was Bear River Smith who showed just how much could be accomplished, with no more than insistent will and gritty determination... and a man's two naked fists.

Chapter XI

Elfego Baca

Huevos Grande! – Standing Alone For Justice

*"Badges? To god-damned hell with badges! We have no badges.
In fact, we don't need badges.
I don' have to show you any steenking badges!"*
-B. Traven (The Treasure of Sierra Madre)

Behold, from out of the spectral dust and obfuscating gun smoke of the past steps the indomitable Elfego Baca, survivor of one of the most uneven gunfights in Western history!

While nearly everyone knows something about Wyatt Earp and the world-famous O.K. Corral, few have heard of S. W. New Mexico's wild

Gila country (pronounced *hee-la*) or the improbable hero of the Frisco siege. Mighty odd, considering that the famous Tombstone shootout rather fairly matched 4 men against 5, consumed about 30 rounds total, and lasted only 1/2 to 3/4 of a minute... whereas the "Frisco War" pitted a single man against a force of 80 to 150 attackers, confrontation lasted over 33 hours! The walls of the flimsy structure where he'd taken refuge were splintered from the constant firing, with one report claiming there were 367 perforations of the door alone. Even forks and knives were hit, with the courtroom audience appropriately aghast at the broom brought in as evidence with 8 bullet holes in its slender handle!

1884 had been a time of increasing hostilities not only between the Apaches and settlers, but also between resident Hispanics and the many newcomers: Celtic-blooded ranchers seeking their own grassy grail. The cowboys packed an assortment of arms including the '73 Winchester lever action repeater in .44-40, and matching .44 caliber single action revolvers courtesy of Samuel Colt. While some of the local Hispanic farmers were as well "heeled," most had nothing but converted surplus muzzleloaders, damascus barreled smoothbores and percussion revolvers from Mexico.

It was in October of that year that a 19 year-old Elfego first heard the alarming stories of how the largely Hispanic community of Frisco was suffering at the hands of a band of often drunken cowpokes, the possible castration of man nicknamed "The Burro," and the roping and beating of one Espitacio Martinez. Supposedly upon hearing that the local Sheriff was doing nothing to help, Baca either helped himself to a Deputy badge out of the reticent lawman's desk drawer, or more likely, purchased a child's toy badge and slapped it on, before strapping on a Colt .45 with its characteristic black resin grips, and riding headlong towards the site of a situation he knew little about.

"Elfego Baca" by Jesse Wolf Hardin

Within a day of his arrival on the 29th, Baca had disarmed and arrested a cowboy named Charlie McCarty, who had decided to celebrate the good life with a shooting spree inside of Milligan's Bar. His prisoner hailed from a notoriously rowdy outfit at the John B. Slaughter ranch, who were none too happy to hear their boy had been snagged by this self-appointed hero. When the local magistrate proved either too hostile or too intimidated to try the case, Baca decided to move McCarty to an adobe house in Middle Plaza for security.

An unpublished photo of Charley McCarty in later years shared by Jewel Derrick Jones, Reserve NM

By this time a dozen or so cowboys had gathered with their Winchester rifles at ready, led by Slaughter foreman Young Parham. They immediately demanded their buddy's release, testing the door and windows with their shoulders. Baca responded from the other side, threatening to shoot if they weren't "out of there by the count of 3." They are said to have been in the process of making jokes about "his type being unable to count" when they heard Baca call out in a single quick breath: "1-2-3!" while he began shooting through the door. In their haste to get some distance between themselves and this unpleasant instruction in rapid arithmetic, Parham's horse reared back and on top of its rider and inflicted damage that would later kill him.

Word of a "Frisco War" promptly spread to the outlying ranches, including those of the well-known James H. Cook and the Englishman, William French. After receiving a signed agreement that he wouldn't be bothered, Baca agreed to allow his prisoner to be "tried" on the following morning at Milligan's Bar. McCarty was fined $5 and released to friends, who almost immediately began to make threatening moves towards Baca. Seeing that he was vulnerable, this would-be Deputy backed out the side door and took over a nearby *jacal*. Made of thin cedar poles stuck into the ground and coated on both sides with an adobe (mud) slip, its walls would offer little resistance to the concerted attack we know followed.

A roper known as Hearne was the first to chance the door, kicking at it and screaming that he'd "get" Baca. He was answered most poignantly by twin 250 grain slugs, one of which caught him solidly in the gut and sent him to the ground. The cowboys responded with what became a steady volley of rifle fire, lobbing rounds from nearly every angle. What the quickly gathering mob failed to realize was that the floor of Baca's insubstantial-looking refuge had been dug down a full foot and a half below ground level. He was thus enabled to coolly return fire with his single-action handguns even as lead rained through the space above.

While most of the town climbed up on the overlooking hills to watch, a group of the attackers stretched blankets between the nearby houses to conceal their movements, and others fired from behind the buttress of the adobe church. One brave attacker fell back with his scalp neatly creased by a bullet, after attempting to approach the *jacal* with an iron stove-door for a shield. Finally as day turned into night, they were able to toss flaming kerosene-soaked rags onto the dirt and latilla (branch) roof. One wall gave way under the combined assault of lead and fire, causing a portion of the roof to collapse on the hapless defender.

Elfego Baca Statue by James Muir, Reserve, NM

They were pretty sure they'd "fixed his wagon" by this time but opted to err on the side of caution, deciding to wait until the following day to try and dig him out. Come the first gray light of dawn they were surprised, mortified even, by the thin wisps of smoke rising from the perforated woodstove. To one end stood a plaster statue of the Nuestra Señora Doña Ana, while at the other end the unruffled Baca nonchalantly flipped his breakfast tortillas! The battle immediately regained its former intensity, with both Elfego and the stoic Señora miraculously unscathed.

Finally, James Cook and the newly arrived Deputy Ross of Socorro convinced Baca to come out, personally guaranteeing his safety. With both guns in hand and every cowboy's rifle trained on his chest, Elfego slowly approached to make his truce. Yes, he would surrender, but only if he could keep his weapons, travel in the back of a buckboard with his and McCarty's Colts, and with all accompanying cowhands keeping at least 30 feet behind them for the entire trip to the Socorro courthouse! The ever-blessed Baca even missed an ambush planned for him on route, when two different groups of avengers each mistakenly thought the other had carried out the mercenary deed. In jail only 4 months, Elfego was tried on 2 separate occasions, and was surprisingly acquitted each time.

It was this episode that earned Elfego his lifelong reputation as a tough hombre, a reputation that followed him throughout his years as a flamboyant criminal lawyer, school superintendent, district attorney, chief bouncer of a Prohibition Era gambling house in Juarez, and a bout as the American agent for General Huerta during the convoluted Mexican revolution. In 1915, Baca turned himself in for shooting down another revolutionary figure, Celestino Otero. While never proven, evidence supported his contention that Otero had fired first, the bullet from a newfangled Savage self-loading pistol piercing the controversial attorney's suit before Baca dropped him with his own .32-20 S&W "Hand-Ejector" model.

Elfego owned and used all kinds of firearms in his lifetime. His favorites were the various Colt Model 1873 single-action revolvers, usually in caliber .45.

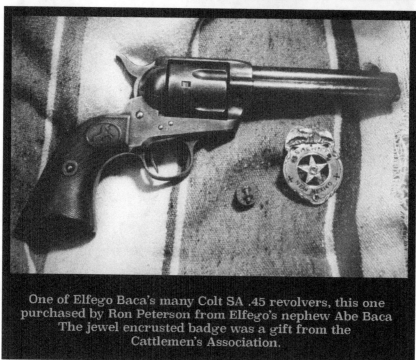

One of Elfego Baca's many Colt SA .45 revolvers, this one purchased by Ron Peterson from Elfego's nephew Abe Baca The jewel encrusted badge was a gift from the Cattlemen's Association.

He also liked to show visitors a custom bolt-action Mauser he says he arranged to have "appropriated" from a disgruntled Pancho Villa. Never one to obey gun laws or any other laws that he didn't believe in, Baca is said to have never gone anywhere – even into a courtroom – without a revolver hidden somewhere on his person. But as much as anything else it was big-bore attitude that Elfego came armed with.

Elfego Baca with the Mauser rifle he said he stole from Pancho Villa

For slightly over 80 years Elfego Baca remained a lively part of New Mexico's cultural landscape, telling spirited stories to anyone with the time to listen. In the year of his birth, horses were the primary means of transportation even in the more civil East, and Winchester's engineers were hard at work on an improvement of their Henry lever-action repeater: the Model 1866 "Yellowboy." He died as 8-cylinder roadsters zoomed by outside his Albuquerque office, on August 27, 1945, exactly 3 weeks following the first wartime deployment of an atomic bomb, and within months of the appearance of the first ball-point pen, the aerosol can and the frozen "T.V. Dinner." By then the M-1 Garrand was in standard use by U.S. troops and precision scoped rifles were fast becoming the norm for stateside hunting.

While a lot has been written about Baca's remarkably good fortune, the trait that best defined him was nerve – or as we call it here in the Southwest, *huevos*. Like other notable Westerners, Elfego set an example for us, not of propriety and submission but an enthusiastic willingness to put excitement and adventure ahead of comfort, and principal ahead of physical safety... accomplishing the seemingly impossible with no more than clear intent, a dependable wheel-gun and unflagging will.

Some years ago I lent my support to the funding and erecting of a life-sized statue of indomitable Elfego. Remote Catron County gets only a smattering of tourists, and only a few of those who stop by the installment take time to read the information on its plaque. As they take turns posing for pictures with their arms around its smooth bronze shoulders, I can't help but think about the need for a since of justice, truth speaking, heartful determination and outright action in our own day and age. If the characters of our past are to provide anything of lasting value, let it not be exciting entertainment and vicarious satisfaction so much as inspiration for us to take a stance and act on our beliefs, heroically taking every risk necessary to do some real and lasting good in this ol' world.

"*In fact, we don't need badges.*"

-B. Traven
(Treasure of Sierra Madre)

Epilogue

"It is not the critic who counts; not the man who points out how the strong man stumbles, or where the doer of deeds could have done them better."
—Theodore Roosevelt (1910)

In the many decades that I've been around, I have become aware of the ways in which law enforcement serves the interests of highly controlling government and the global *corporados* pulling its strings. As a young runaway on the streets in the 1960s I was harassed and provoked by the authorities. While I wasn't caught and made to pay for most of the crazy things that I did, I was nonetheless framed and arrested for things I *didn't* do. I watched the beatings of people protesting the ill-conceived Viet Nam War, and then was held down and sprayed with mace for calling attention to the clearcutting of the last Redwoods. I can't help but note that law enforcement agencies are being increasingly militarized, trained to quell the unrest of rightfully distressed citizens, and employed to protect the financial elite from the average working folk who understandably feel they aren't getting a fair deal.

At the same time, I dealt with enough heartless predators, brutal thugs and pistol toting gangs back then to doubt people would be any safer without the presence of men and women patrolling and monitoring our cities. Even as an outlaw biker, I made friends with honorable lawmen who proved nearly as wild and self-directed as me. In more recent times, the Sheriffs of my home county of Catron, for example, have proven remarkable, and often laudable, in their individualistic interpretation and enforcement of the law. Shawn, our current badge wearer as I pen these words, is undeniably, impeccably honest. He not only doesn't harass anyone, he looks out for the safety and well being of the people of this area in a very personal and committed way. While I am confident he would slap leather and shoot it out with any ne'er-do-well who was caught hurting people, he has proven to be the epitome of what was once called a "Peace Officer" – doing his best to ensure the peace and well being of our liberty loving residents.

Robo cops aside, lawmen are human, with a mix of traits and qualities, haunted by the same temptations as everyone else, weighing choices based on their experiences, duties, and beliefs. They are different in at least one way, however, from most of rest of modern humanity: Their career and service puts them into mortal danger on a daily basis, even in the most friendly of rural towns. Their motivations, which are most often to benefit their communities, have them risking their lives. While we hear of fewer crimes and shootouts that are either as interesting or commendable as some Old West altercations, there is actually more danger in many sections of our cities today than there ever was back when men carried their Colts openly in the saloons of Denver and Deadwood, Tucson and Albuquerque. And no matter what each officer's good or bad deeds, no matter what laws they enforce or break, it often remains the people who risk the most that make the biggest impressions on us. Regardless of the wisdom of many wars, we look up to soldiers putting it all on the line. In spite of the medical system's pushing of harmful pharmaceuticals and the disparity in access, we nonetheless respect any doctors we hear about tackling serious outbreaks of communicable disease, firemen knocking down a burning door to save a child trapped inside, and the lawmen taking chances.

"The credit belongs to the man who is actually in the arena, whose face is marred by dust and sweat and blood; who strives valiantly; who errs, who comes short again and again, because there is no effort without error and shortcoming; but who does actually strive to do the deeds; who knows great enthusiasms, the great devotions; who spends himself in a worthy cause; who at the best knows in the end the triumph of high achievement, and who at the worst, if he fails, at least fails while daring greatly, so that his place shall never be with those cold and timid souls who neither know victory nor defeat."

–Theodore Roosevelt (1910)

The eleven colorful men profiled herein, should all be examples to us – both positive and negative examples. The tales of some seemingly unsavory acts can reinforce in us what not to do, and make us even stronger in our determination to be ethical and act in ways that we can be proud of. So can the examples of what appears to us to be heroism. And it is up to each of us to determine for our own selves what is deplorable and what is commendable, what to oppose and what to support, which laws are worthy of being adhered to and which deserve and even require our well meaning disobedience.

As I bring this book to completion, I pause to look out the window of our cabin at the cottonwood trees swaying above the river. I scan the hillside for sign of any of the elk, deer, turkey, bear and other assorted creatures often seen there. After a few minutes of what can only be described as pure reverie, my eyes settle on the sight of a large raven, first circling only 20 yards from where I sit in my antique writer's chair, but then flying in ever larger circles in the impossibly blue New Mexico skies. I crane my head upwards, turning my head slightly from side to side, following the silhouette of this free bird with my entire being.... climbing higher than these Saliz Mountains, appearing smaller and smaller until completely out of sight.

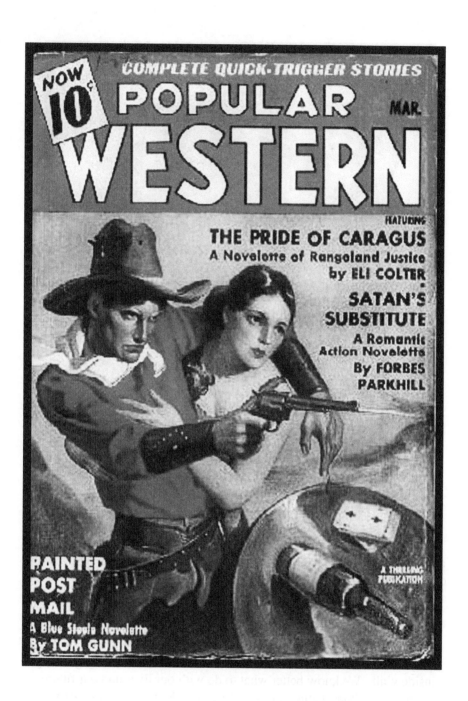

Acknowledgments

I am happy to express here my gratitude, first to my loving and supportive family. To the people of the rural West who embody and strive to pass on to others an abiding love for the Old Ways, and to the citizens of backwoods Catron County.

Thanks especially to every tireless researcher and well meaning writer whose work I have ever read. From the reporters writing for the newspapers of the 1800s to the historical book authors of today. Some such accounts are factual, some complete fiction, and most a reasonable mix, but all have been inspiration and fodder for my own explorations and extrapolations. Thanks to Bob Boze Bell of True West Magazine for doing so much to keep the campfires going and the dark woods of history in the light. And especially to my pards Boge Quinn and John Taffin for their great Foreword and Introduction to this undoubtedly flawed work.

Hats off, as well, to every lover, writer and reader of the tales of the inimitable American frontier, with a bit of the wild and wooly growing inside y'all. We know better what to do with our lives and our future, thanks to an honest study of those lives and doin's that came before.

"Marshall Commodore Perry Owens"
by Jesse Wolf Hardin

About The Author

Author Jesse Wolf Hardin is the cofounder of the acclaimed Plant Healer Magazine (www.PlantHealerMagazine.com) with a focus on empowering herbalism and natural medicine for the people. His hundreds of published articles and over a dozen books have helped stretch as well as entertain his readers on topics as diverse as healing practices, natural history and the history of the West, sense of place, American history, contemporary politics, primitive hunting and antique firearms... always with a message such as increased awareness, the wisdom of the land, personal responsibility and a code of honor.

Books by Hardin include <u>Old Guns & Whispering Ghosts</u> for history buffs and gun collectors, <u>21st Century Herbalists</u>, an historical novel of the Southwest circa 1916 <u>The Medicine Bear</u>, <u>The Plant Healer's Path</u> , and a volume of essays filled with rural humor, sentiment and attitude: <u>Pancho Villa's Motorcycle</u>.

"Hardin has a fascinating style.... almost lyrical.
His perspective on the Old West is both romantic and dramatic.
I spent some of my formative years long ago on the banks of the
Cimarron River listening to Navaho storytellers relate tales of their
ancestors and the history of that part of New Mexico.
Jesse's writing is worthy of those fascinating chronicles."
-Ned Schwing Krause Pub. author and editor

"....you feel and demonstrate the polar opposites bound up together in
one self, and they struggle inside one heart and skull.... and it is this
twist, the resultant continuous twist in the gut of this relentless "love of
things unreconcilable" which provides the lava, the moving
power of great Lit." **-Barbara Mor**

The author sincerely welcomes your letters of appreciation, speaking offers, and any disparaging remarks... sent to:
Scribe@OldWestScribe.com

www.OldWestScribe.com

May you rise to every challenge, enjoy every adventure, & savor every good deed you ever do.

CPSIA information can be obtained at www.ICGtesting.com
Printed in the USA
LVOW05s1539250914

405880LV00022B/1148/P

9 781499 650174